Mark Twain's Guide to Heidelberg

His journey through Germany in 1878

EDITED BY WERNER PIEPER

WERNER PIEPER'S MEDIENXPERIMENTE

Excerpts from "A Tramp Abroad" by Mark Twain
Sources of original words by Mark Twain (all quotes are numbered):

1. Mark Twain's Notebooks & Journals, Volume II (1877-1833).
   University of California Press, 1975.
2. A. B. Paine: Mark Twain, A Biography. Harper & Brothers.
3. Frank Baldanza: Mark Twain, An Introduction and Interpretation.
   Barnes & Noble, New York, 1961.
4. Charles Neider: The Autobiography of Mark Twain. Harper & Row, New York
5. Mark Twain's Letters to his Publishers, 1867-1894; ed. H. Hill.
   University of California Press, 1967.
6. Mark Twain's Notebooks & Journals, Vol. III (1883-1891); ed. F. Anderson et al.
   University of California Press, 1979.
7. Mark Twain/Howells – Letters, 1872-1910; ed. H. N. Smith and W. M. Gibson.
   The Belknap Press of Harvard University Press, Cambridge, Mass., 1960.
8. Mark Twain's Autobiography, Vol. I; ed. A. B. Paine. Harper & Brothers Publ.,
   New York, London, 1924.
9. Mark Twain Speaking; ed. Paul Fatout. University of Iowa Press.
10. Mark Twain's Letters, Vol. I; ed. A. B. Paine. Harper & Brothers Publishers,
    New York and London.
11. Edgar Hemminghaus: Mark Twain in Germany. Ams Press Inc., London, 1940;
    reprinted 1966 NY.
12. Günter Möhle: Das Europabild Mark Twains. Junker und Dünnhaupt Verlag, Berlin, 1940.
13. Albert B. Paine: Mark Twain's Notebook. Harper & Brothers Publishers,
    New York and London, 1935.
14. Mark Twain in Heidelberg, with commentary by Harry B. Davis.
    Verlag Brausdruck Heidelberg, 1985 (= excerpts from "A Tramp Abroad").
15. Heinz F. Friedrichs: President Dwight D. Eisenhowers Ancestors and Relations.
    Verlag Degener, Neustadt near Nürnberg, 1955.

Editor of this edition:
Werner Pieper, who did the research,
wrote commentaries and put the appendice together.
Typesetting: Petra Petzold, Heidelberg
Helpers: Micky Remann, Jane X. England, Daniel Dragmanli
Title picture by Michel Meyer
Photos on pages 14/15, 77, 121, by Richard Maychrzak
Printed by Maro Druck, Augsburg

Published by
Werner Pieper's MedienXperimente
Alte Schmiede
D-69488 Löhrbach
Fax (++49) 0 62 01 - 2 25 85

ISBN 3-922708-12-9

CONTENTS

ABOUT THIS BOOK

Coming to Europe in 1878, Samuel Langhorne Clemens, alias Mark Twain, was already a famous man. His book "Innocents Abroad" – and not the already published "Tom Sawyer" – was the foundation of his fame. It was the most popular travel book in the States at that time. Readers liked his way of questioning the (old) culture of the Old World. He asked himself "What should I do in Europe?" He didn't know much about history and was full of prejudice. But because he applies his witty scepticism not only to Europe, but to himself as well – he knew that an American visitor abroad might look strange to local people! – his book "A Tramp Abroad", from which large parts of this book are taken, still is a great caricature of modern tourism.

"A Tramp Abroad" was his second travel book. Here he appears to look down on Europe like the classical American Imperialist. But where his measurement seems to be all American, his humor is definitely British.

As the editor of this edition I thought about having my comments etc. translated into perfect English, but then I thought of Twain's struggles with the German language and decided to stick to my pidgin-English to give you a few smiles while reading this, knowing Mark Twain would have loved it this way.

His method of writing was to start several books at the same time. Then his energy left him, before he could finish any of them. When "Tom Sawyer" didn't turn out to be as successful as he had hoped he turned to other areas of life: he married his wife Livy. But marriage didn't help to end the "creative block". He decided to come to Europe to finish all the books he had started. He was looking for a quiet place, where people didn't know him, and he wanted to write a book about traveling that people would actually read.

He found the place he was looking for in his writing room in the inn up on the Königstuhl mountain. He wrote parts of "A Tramp Abroad" there, but destroyed most of his manuscripts later and re-wrote the book in München in the following winter. He worked on "Huckleberry Finn" as well, most likely on chapter 16:

"This experience of the Neckar Valley was enough to trigger Twain's fantasy, and a raft voyage was conjured up. Twain's biographer Justin Kaplan believes the mythical raft voyage to be crucial; he sees it as a parody of Huck and Jim's voyage down the Mississippi – an attempt at breaking the block which had stalled Twain's work on 'Huckleberry Finn.' If that is true, we could have

Heidelberg to thank for one of the greatest novels in American literature." *(14)* Twain wrote several versions of "A Tramp Abroad." When he finished it on November 11th, 1879, he had to take 1,400 of his 4,000 handwritten pages out. "A Tramp Abroad" was published in the States on March 13th, 1880 and shortly after that in Germany, too.

The original "A Tramp Abroad" contains 50 chapters and 6 appendices. For this edition I have concentrated on his time in Heidelberg, which fills almost half of the original book. I have tried to find all additional notes he wrote about Heidelberg in his note books, the letters to his friends, to family and publishers, travel diaries and other sources. All these additional texts are added as side-notes.

To make it as easy as possible for you to walk in Twain's Heidelberg foot steps, I have added information about some of the hotels and places Twain went to that still exist. I have given telephone numbers for you to check opening times and hotel rates where possible.

At the end of the book you will find more background information about Mark Twain in Germany and a short history of the relationship between Heidelberg and the U.S.A. I can promise you a big surprise there...

Lots of people helped me in doing the research for this background information, they are all listed in the German edition of this book, "Mark Twain – ein Amerikaner in Heidelberg."

Special thanks for this edition go to Mr. Dressler, the press officer of the American Army in Heidelberg, Micky Remann and Jane X. England for proof reading.

Last but not least thanks to Samuel Langhorne Clemens, the man himself. Maybe it was really his influence that saved Heidelberg from being bombed during World War II.

I hope this book makes you realize that you are not the first American to feel the special spirit of Heidelberg. May you enjoy this book and the city as much as Mark Twain did. Start by walking up to the Königstuhl ...

Werner Pieper, Editor

Heidelberg, May 6th, 1995
(exactly 117 years after Twain came to town
and 50 years after World War II ended ...)

TO THE READER

Perhaps you were about to say that formerly I went Abroad as an Innocent, but that this time, fortified with experience and guile, I went Abroad as a Tramp. (But that inference would not be quite right, while at the same time it would not be wholly) Let us not argue this question. When I chose my book's title, I only intended it to describe the nature of my journey, which was a *walk*, through foreign lands, – that is, a tramp; but the more I think of how little I cared whither I went, or how long it took me to go, or whether I saw anything or found out anything when I got there, so long as I had a lazy, delightful, irresponsible high-holiday time on the road, the more I perceived that in using the word Tramp I was unconsciously describing the walker as well as the walk. Very well, let it go at that. Tramps are increasing; by and by they may be in the majority; in that day a Tramp will be elected President of the United States: I seem to have a future before me.

I went abroad to visit some countries which I had not seen before. I meant to traverse them on foot. It was a vast undertaking, but I believed that by getting a little lift here and there when I was pretty tired, I could accomplish it. If I succeeded, I should have something to boast of as long as I lived; I should be admired and looked up to as a man who had conceived and carried out one of the most formidable projects of the age.

But I meant to have a good time, just the same, and I had it. I had been at work a long time; I was not going to walk to tire myself, but to rest myself. I was off for a satisfying, comprehensive, and elaborate holiday, – a holiday in the open air, rather than in cities and picture galleries.

I had a couple of light minor purposes, also: to acquire the German language, and to perfect myself in Art. *(5)*

Mark Twain

Paris, July, 1879.

FRANKFORT

One day it occured to me that it had been many years since the world had been afforded the spectacle of a man adventurous enough to undertake a journey through Europe on foot. After much thought, I decided that I was a person fitted to furnish to mankind this spectacle. So I determined to do it. This was in March, 1878.

I looked about me for the right sort of person to accompany me in the capacity of agent, and finally hired a Mr. Harris for this service.

It was also my purpose to study art while in Europe. Mr. Harris was in sympathy with me in this. He was as much of an enthusiast in art as I was, and not less anxious to learn to paint. I desired to learn the German language; so did Harris.

Toward the middle of April we sailed in the *Holsatia*, Captain Brandt, and had a very pleasant trip, indeed.

After a brief rest at Hamburg, we made preparations for a long pedestrian trip southward in the soft spring weather, but at the last moment we changed the programme, for private reasons, and took the express train.

Mark Twain and his family – Mrs. Clemens, and their two little girls, Clara and Susy – accompanied by Miss Clara Spaulding of Elmira, N. Y. (later Mrs. John B. Stanchfield) sailed on the *Holsatia* for Hamburg, April 11, 1878. *(13)*

17th April a most remarkable day – frequent hail, sleet, snow & wind-squalls, with dark lowering Himmel, und mit hölle Sonnenschein zwichen. Sehr hohe See-wellen, mit blenden grün in dem zerbrochenen Spitze. *(1)*

An exceedingly steady ship in an ordinary sea is the *Holsatia* – rolls very little.

Noisy cabin – shrieking children – the ceaseless metallic clatter of that old cracked kettle of a piano and the thunder and pounding of the screw, with an occasional avalanche of crashing crockery as the ship lurches, this is the afternoon hell in this ship daily. But the piano is the special hell – how it racks one's head.

Until it stops – then you think the scream-voiced boy is it.

There goes the B's crying baby. Now a guffaw of beastly laughter. Now the little Spanish boy is hurled headlong down into our gangway by a lurch of the ship and fetches up with a heavy bang and pile of books and rubbish tumble down.

20th April. Three days of heavy sea now and the above is my first attempt to get an afternoon nap.

It is a marvel that never loses its surprise by repetition, this aiming a ship at a mark 3000 miles away and hitting the bull's-eye in a fog – as we did. When the fog fell on us the captain said we ought to be at such and such a spot (it had been 18 hours since an observation was taken) with the Scilly Islands bearing so and so, and about so many miles away. Hove the lead and got 48 fathoms – looked on the chart and sure enough this depth of water showed that we were right where the captain said we were. Another idea. For ages man probably did not know why God carpeted the ocean bottom with sand in one place, shells in another etc. But we see, now; the kind of bottom the lead brings up shows where a ship is when the soundings don't – and also it confirms the soundings. *(13)*

Goethe's house – the courier had the effrontery to propose we visit birthplace of Rothschild. My dear sir, 2 or 300 years ago, they'd have skinned this Jew in old Frankfort, instead of paying homage to his birthplace – but it is an advance – we have quit loathing Jews & gone to worshiping their money. – Come, let us exhibit the birthplaces of Vanderbilt & Stewart to admiring foreigners. *(1)*

The Portier is a most useful & wonderful being. He starts as waiter, then head waiter, then Portier, then gets a hotel of his own. – Speaks 5 or 6 languages. Let somebody else say this. *(1)*

The clerk of a first class hotel in America accomplishes everything you can possibly desire – & that is what the German portier does – but there is this difference – if the clerk chooses, he can clog & slight you, but the portier can't afford that, or his fees would suffer.

Was told that the portier of one great Berlin Hotel paid $500 a year (not *marks,* but $) for his place. *(1)*

We made a short halt at Frankfort-on-the-Main, and found it an interesting city. I would have liked to visit the birthplace of Gutenberg, but it could not be done, as no memorandum of the site of the house has been kept. So we spent an hour in the Goethe mansion instead. The city permits this house to belong to private parties, instead of gracing and dignifying herself with the honor of possessing and protecting it.

Frankfort is one of the sixteen cities which have the distinction of being the place where the following incident occured. Charlemagne, while chasing the Saxons (as *he* said), or being chased by them (as *they* said), arrived at the bank of the river at dawn, in a fog. The enemy were either before him or behind him; but in any case he wanted to get across, very badly. He would have given anything for a guide, but none was to be had. Presently he saw a deer, followed by her young, approach the water. He watched her, judging that she would seek a ford, and he was right. She waded over, and the army followed. So a great Frankish victory or defeat was gained or avoided; and in order to commemorate the episode, Charlemagne commanded a city to be built there, which he named Frankfort, – the ford of the Franks. None of the other cities where this event happened were named from it. This is good evidence that Frankfort was the first place it occurred at.

Frankfort has another distinction, – it is the birthplace of the German alphabet; or at least of the German word for alphabet, – *Buchstaben*. They say that the first movable types were made on birch sticks, – *Buchstabe*, – hence the name.

I was taught a lesson in political economy in Frankfort. I had brought from home a box containing a thousand very cheap cigars. By way of experiment, I stepped into a little shop in a queer old back street, took four gaily decorated boxes of wax matches and three cigars, and laid down a silver piece worth 48 cents. The man gave me 43 cents change.

In Frankfort everybody wears clean clothes, and I think we noticed that this strange thing was the case in Hamburg, too, and in the villages along the road. Even in the narrowest and poorest and most ancient quarters of Frankfort neat and clean clothes were the rule. The little children of both sexes were nearly always nice enough to take into a body's lap. And as for the uniforms of the soldiers, they were newness and brightness carried to perfection. One could never detect a smirch or a grain of dust upon them. The street car conductors and drivers wore pretty uniforms which seemed to be just out of the bandbox, and their manners were as fine as their clothes.

In one of the shops I had the luck to stumble upon a book which has charmed me nearly to death. It is entitled "The Legends of the Rhine from Basle to Rotterdam, by F. J. Kiefer; Translated by L. W. Garnham, B.A." All tourists *mention* the Rhine legends, – in that sort of way which quietly pretends that the mentioner has been familiar with them all his life, and that the reader cannot possibly be ignorant of them, – but no tourist ever *tells* them. So this little book fed me in a very hungry place; and I, in my turn, intend to feed my reader, with one or two little lunches from the same larder. I shall not mar Garnham's translation by meddling with its English; for the most toothsome thing about it is its quaint fashion of building English sentences on the German plan, – and punctuating them according to no plan at all.

In the chapter devoted to "Legends of Frankfort," I find the following:

"THE KNAVE OF BERGEN."

"In Frankfort at the Romer was a great maskball, at the coronation festival, and in the illuminated saloon, the clanging music invited to dance, and splendidly appeared the rich toilets and charms of the ladies, and the festively costumed Princes and Knights. All seemed pleasure, joy, and roguish gayety, only one of the numerous guests had a gloomy exterior; but exactly the black armor in which he walked about excited general attention, and his tall figure, as well as the noble propriety of his movements, attracted especially the regards of the ladies. Who the Knight was? Nobody could guess, for his Vizier was well closed, and nothing made him recognizable. Proud and yet modest he advanced to the Empress; bowed on one knee before her seat, and begged for the favor of a waltz with the Queen of the festival. And she allowed his request. With light and graceful steps he danced through the long saloon, with the sovereign who thought never to have found a more dexterous and excellent dancer. But also by the grace of his manner, and fine conversation he knew to win the Queen, and she graciously accorded him a second dance for which he begged, a third, and a fourth, as well as others were not refused to him. How all regarded the happy dancer, how many envied him the high favor; how increased curiosity, who the masked knight could be.

"Also the Emperor became more and more excited with curiosity, and with great suspense one awaited the hour, when according to mask-law, each masked guest must make himself known. This moment came, but although all others had unmasked; the secret knight still refused to allow his features to be seen, till at last the Queen driven by curiosity, and vexed at the obstinate refusal; commanded him to open his Vizier. He opened it, and none of the high ladies and knights knew him. But from the crowded spectators, 2 officials advanced, who recognized the black dancer, and horror and terror spread in the saloon, as they said who the supposed knight was. It was the executioner of Bergen. But glowing with rage, the King commanded to seize the criminal and lead him to death, who had ventured to dance, with the queen; so disgraced the Empress, and insulted the crown. The culpable threw himself at the feet of the Emperor, and said, –

"'Indeed I have heavily sinned against all noble guests assembled here, but most heavily against you my sovereign and my queen. The Queen is insulted by my haughtiness equal to treason, but no punishment even blood, will not be able to wash out the disgrace, which you have suffered by me. Therefore oh King! allow me to propose a remedy, to efface the shame, and to render it as if not done. Draw your sword and knight me, then I will throw down my gauntlet, to every one who dares to speak disrespectfully of my king.'

"The Emperor was surprised at this bold proposal, however it appeared the wisest to him; 'You are a knave,' he replied after a moment's consideration, 'however your advice is good, and displays prudence, as your offense shows adventurous courage. Well then,' and gave him the knight-stroke, 'so I raise you to nobility, who begged for grace for your offense now kneels before me, rise as knight; knavish you have acted, and Knave of Bergen shall you be called henceforth,' and gladly the Black knight rose; three cheers were given in honor of the Emperor, and loud cries of joy testified the approbation with which the Queen danced still once with the Knave of Bergen."

THE HOME OF THE MONSTER – BURG FRANKENSTEIN.

Write a burlesque Frankenstein – (Freestone). His uncle a bonanza simpleton, good & kind. F. has no memory on *Tuesdays,* but can't notice it himself because he can't remember then that there *is* such a day as Tuesday. Engages himself to girls on that day, forgetting previous one – appoints a dozen weddings for a Tuesday & goes off fishing. *(7)*

We don't know if Twain went to see Burg Frankenstein, the "Home of the monster" to be inspired to write about Frankenstein, but he probably did. You can get inspired too. Burg Frankenstein is en route from Heidelberg to Frankfurt Airport. Contact: Burg Frankenstein, **64367 Mühltal**, tel. 06151 / 54618. It houses a restaurant, a café on the terrace and wine is served from the cellars of the real Frankenstein family. They arrange special parties each year on Halloween with real horror and monster shows, with campfires and lots of surprises.

HEIDELBERG

We stopped at a hotel by the railway station. Next morning, as we sat in my room waiting for breakfast to come up, we got a good deal interested in something which was going on over the way, in front of another hotel. First, the personage who is called the *portier* (who is not the *porter*, but is a sort of first-mate of a hotel) appeared at the door in a spick and span new blue cloth uniform, decorated with shining brass buttons, and with bands of gold lace around his cap and wristbands; and he wore white gloves, too. He shed an official glance upon the situation, and then began to give orders. Two women servants came out with pails and brooms and brushes, and gave the sidewalk a thorough scrubbing; meanwhile two others scrubbed the four marble steps which led up to the door; beyond these we could see some men-servants taking up the carpet of the grand staircase. This carpet was carried away and the last grain of dust beaten and banged and swept out of it; then brought back and put down again. The brass stair rods received an exhaustive polishing and were returned to their places. Now a troop of servants brought pots and tubs of blooming plants and formed them into a beautiful jungle about the door and the base of the staircase. Other servants adorned all the balconies of the various stories with flowers and banners; others ascended to the roof and hoisted a

great flag on a staff there. Now came some more chambermaids and retouched the sidewalk, and afterward wiped the marble steps with damp cloths and finished by dusting them off with feather brushes. Now a broad black carpet was brought out and laid down the marble steps and out across the sidewalk to the curbstone. The *portier* cast his eye along it, and found it was not absolutely straight; he commanded it to be straightened; the servants made the effort, – made several efforts, in fact, – but the *portier* was not satisfied. He finally had it taken up, and then he put it down himself and got it right.

At this stage of the proceedings, a narrow bright red carpet was unrolled and stretched from the top of the marble steps to the curbstone, along the center of the black carpet. This red path cost the *portier* more trouble than even the black one had done. But he patiently fixed and re-fixed it until it was exactly right and lay precisely in the middle of the black carpet. In New York these performances would have gathered a mighty crowd of curious and intensely interested spectators; but here it only captured an audience of half-a-dozen little boys, who stood in a row across the pavement, some with their school knapsacks on their backs and their hands in their pockets, others with arms full of bundles, and all absorbed in the show. Occasionally one of them skipped irreverently over the carpet and took up a position on the other side. This always visibly annoyed the *portier*.

Now came a waiting interval. The landlord, in plain clothes, and bare-headed, placed himself on the bottom marble step, abreast the *portier*, who stood on the other end of the same steps; six or eight waiters, gloved, bare-

headed, and wearing their whitest linen, their whitest cravats, and their finest swallow-tails, grouped themselves about these chiefs, but leaving the carpet-way clear. Nobody moved or spoke any more but only waited.

In a short time the shrill piping of a coming train was heard, and immediately groups of people began to gather in the street. Two or three open carriages arrived, and deposited some maids of honor and some male officials at the hotel. Presently another open carriage brought the Grand Duke of Baden, a stately man in uniform, who wore the handsome brass-mounted, steel-spiked helmet of the army on his head. Last came the Empress of Germany and the Grand Duchess of Baden in a close carriage; these passed through the low-bowing groups of servants and disappeared in the hotel, exhibiting to us only the backs of their heads, and then the show was over.

It appears to be as difficult to land a monarch as it is to launch a ship.[3]

But as to Heidelberg. The weather was growing pretty warm, – very warm, in fact. So we left the valley and took quarters at the Schloss Hotel, on the hill, above the Castle.

Heidelberg lies at the mouth of a narrow gorge – a gorge the shape of a shepherd's crook; if one looks up it he perceives that it is about straight, for a mile and a half, then makes a sharp curve to the right and disappears. This gorge, – along whose bottom pours the swift Neckar, – is confined between (or cloven through) a couple of long, steep ridges, a thousand feet high and densely wooded clear to their summits, with the exception of one section which has been shaved and put under cultivation. These ridges are chopped off at the mouth of the gorge and form two bold and conspicuous headlands, with Heidelberg nestling between them; from their bases spreads away the vast dim expanse of the Rhine valley, and into this expanse the Neckar goes wandering in shining curves and is presently lost to view.

Now if one turns and looks up the gorge once more, he will see the Schloss Hotel on the right, perched on a precipice overlooking the Neckar, – a precipice which is so sumptuously cushioned and draped with foliage that no glimpse of the rock appears. The building seems very airily situated. It has the appearance of being on a shelf half way up the wooded mountain side; and as it is remote and isolated, and very white, it makes a strong mark against the lofty leafy rampart at its back.

This hotel had a feature which was a decided novelty, and one which might be adopted with advantage by any house which is perched in a commanding situation. This feature may be described as a series of glass-enclosed parlors *clinging to the outside of the house,* one against each and every bed-chamber and drawing-room. They are like long, narrow, high-ceiled bird-cages hung against

"The Schloss Hotel had been built seven years earlier as competition for the best hotels down in the city. It was accustomed to celebrities. Richard Wagner had stayed there the year before, 1877, and so had, ironically, Ulysses S. Grant, whose corrupt administration hat inspired Twain's book *The Guilded Age*. Grant had just left office and was on a world tour. He and Wagner met in the hotel lobby, but little came of the encounter." *(14)*

The Schloss Hotel was one of the most beautifully located hotels in Germany of that time. Twain booked a 250 Dollar a month suite. The hotel was rebuilt in the '30s, and since the '60s it's been used as an international student dormitory. The photographer, Richard Staatenlos, who took the photograph of Heidelberg today seen through Twain's old window, met two students from India and Nepal who where living in Twain's old rooms when he visited then. The Schloss Hotel is easy to spot from anywhere in the Old Town: just look up to the Schloss and let your eyes wander on the same height to the left corner of the mountain, just on the edge to the Neckar valley.

[Part of letter to W. D. Howells, in Boston:]

SHLOSS-HOTEL HEIDELBERG, Sunday, a.m., May 26, 1878.

My dear Howells, –

... divinely located. From this airy porch among the shining groves we look down upon Heidelberg Castle, and upon the swift Neckar, and the town, and out over the wide green level of the Rhine valley – a marvelous prospect. We are in a cul-de-sac formed of hill-ranges and river; we are on the side of a steep mountain; the river at our feet is walled, on its other side, (yes, on both sides,) by a steep and wooded mountain-range which rises abruptly aloft from the water's edge; portions of these mountains are densely wooded; the plain of the Rhine, seen through the mouth of this pocket, has many and peculiar charms for the eye.

Our bedroom has two great glass bird-cages (enclosed balconies) one looking towards the Rhine valley and sunset, the other looking up the Neckar cul-de-sac, and naturally we spend nearly all our time in these – when one is sunny the other is shady. We have tables and chairs in them; we do our reading, writing, studying, smoking and suppering in them.

The view from these bird-cages is my despair. The pictures change from one enchanting aspect to another in ceaseless procession, never keeping one form half an hour, and never taking on an unlovely one.

And then Heidelberg on a dark night! It is massed, away down there, almost right under us, you know, and stretches off toward the valley. Its curved and interlacing streets are a cobweb, beaded thick with lights – a wonderful thing to see; then the rows of lights on the arched bridges, and their glinting reflections in the water; and away at the far end, the Eisenbahnhof, with its twenty solid acres of glittering gas-jets, a huge garden, as one may say, whose every plant is a flame.

These balconies are the darlingest things. I have spent all the morning in this north one. Counting big and little, it has 256 panes of glass in it; so one is in effect right out in the free sunshine, and yet sheltered from wind and rain – and likewise doored and curtained from whatever may be going on in the bedroom. It must have been a noble genius who devised this hotel. Lord, how blessed is the repose, the tranquillity of this place! Only two sounds; the happy clamor of the birds in the groves, and the muffled music of the Neckar, tumbling over the opposing dykes. It is no hardship to lie awake awhile, nights, for this subdued roar has exactly the sound of a steady rain beating upon a roof. It is so healing to the spirit; and it bears up the thread of one's imaginings as the accompaniment bears up a song.

The hotel grounds join and communicate with the Castle grounds; so we and the children loaf in the winding paths of those leafy vastnesses a great deal, and drink beer and listen to excellent music. *(10)*

the building. My room was a corner room, and had two of these things, a north one and a west one.

From the north cage one looks up the Neckar gorge; from the west one he looks down it. This last affords the most extensive view, and it is one of the loveliest that can be imagined, too. Out of a billowy upheaval of vivid green foliage, a rifle-shot removed, rises the huge ruin of Heidelberg Castle, with empty window arches, ivy-mailed battlements, moldering towers – the Lear of inanimate nature, – deserted, discrowned, beaten by the storms, but royal still, and beautiful. It is a fine sight to see the evening sunlight suddenly strike the leafy declivity at the Castle's base and dash up it and drench it as with a luminous spray, while the adjacent groves are in deep shadow.

Behind the Castle swells a great dome-shaped hill, forest-clad, and beyond that a nobler and loftier one. The Castle looks down upon the compact brown-roofed town; and from the town two picturesque old bridges span the river. Now the view broadens; through the gateway of the sentinel headlands you gaze out over the wide Rhine plain, which stretches away, softly and richly tinted, grows gradually and dreamily indistinct, and finally melts imperceptibly into the remote horizon.

I have never enjoyed a view which had such a serene and satisfying charm about it as this one gives.

The first night we were there, we went to bed and to sleep early; but I awoke at the end of two or three hours, and lay a comfortable while listening to the soothing patter of the rain against the balcony windows. I took to to be rain, but it turned out to be only the murmur of the restless Neckar, tumbling over her dikes and dams far below, in the gorge. I got up and went into the west balcony and saw a wonderful sight. Away down on the level, under the black mass of the Castle, the town lay, stretched along the river, its intricate cob-web of streets jeweled with twinkling lights; there were rows of lights on the bridges; these flung lances of light upon the water, in the black shadows of the arches; and away at the extremity of all this fairy spectacle blinked and glowed a massed multitude of gas jets which seemed to cover acres of ground; it was as if all the diamonds in the world had been spread out there. I did not know before, that a half mile of sextuple railway tracks could be made such an adorn-ment.

One thinks Heidelberg by day – with its surroundings – is the last possibil-ity of the beautiful; but when he sees Heidelberg by night, a fallen Milky Way, with that glittering railway constellation pinned to the border, he requires time to consider upon the verdict.

One never tires of poking about in the dense woods that clothe all these lofty Neckar hills to their tops. The great deeps of a boundless forest have a beguiling and impressive charm in any country; but German legends and fairy tales have given these an added charm. They have peopled all that region with gnomes, and dwarfs, and all sorts of mysterious and uncanny creatures. At the time I am writing of, I had been reading so much of this literature that sometimes I was not sure but I was beginning to believe in the gnomes and fairies as realities.

The photo shows the old railway station on the left and Hotel Schrieder on the right. The Clemens family stayed here on their first night in Heidelberg. The railway station was rebuilt and relocated one mile to the west in the fifties. Hotel Schrieder became the Heidelberg Holiday Inn in 1988. Tel. 06221 / 9170.

Apart from his diary entries, the only definite proof of Mark Twain staying in Heidelberg is a little note in the local paper "Heidelberger Zeitung" from May 7th, 1878, which just mentions his stay in this hotel. All the old documents of the Hotel Schrieder disappeared after 1945, when the U.S. Army confiscated the hotel. It was given back to the German owners in 1966.

May 28 – Another curious sunset. Blazing hot sun approaching the top of the Heiligenberg – all the mountains beyond the plains shut utterly out by an interposed dead leaden sky – (all the plain between vague & indistinct) a hole in the horizon-edge of that leaden sky just over the slop of the Heiligenberg & in that hole 2 tall black factory chimneys 20 miles away, in the plain, pouring out black smoke. Have often seen what looked like spectral chimneys there, shadowy & indistinct, but now they are black as ink & strongly defined & are sending off long streamers of black smoke & grey. The little patch of Rhine to their right under the horizon, shines strong & clear. – No air stirring in Heidelberg – as I look down on its old dark brown roofs, I see them through a curling & twisting pale blue veil of smoke-wreaths which there is no wind to blow away. The effect is exceedingly odd, & very pretty. *(1)*

June 2, '78, ten days ago a socialist fired 4 shots at the emperor, in Berlin, without effect. He was captured. The emperor was driving out with his daughter, the Grand Duchess of Baden.

Today he was fired upon again, this time by an under officer of the government, it was said. Wounded in cheek and arm he lost a good deal of blood. He is so old the shock may kill him. A crowd rushed at the house and were received with a shot from the assassin which hit a landlord. The assassin wounded himself, but not fatally.

June 10, Emperor to leave his bed again – this is wonderful. 8 days after receiving such lacerating wounds in arm, shoulder and side – with buckshot – and at his age [William I, then 81 years old]. *(13)*

Rented and paid for a room for a month at the pretty little Wirtschaft (i. e., inn) under the Königstuhl. My work-den is in the second story of a little Wirtschaft that stands at the base of the tower on the summit of the Königstuhl. I walk up there every morning, at 10, write until 3, talk the most hopeless and improbable German with the family till 5, then tramp down to the Hotel for the night." *(1)*

The inn on top of the Königstuhl mountain ("The King's Chair"), the highest point of Heidelberg, was built in 1864. Call 21607 if you want to rent a room up there, even if Twain's room is gone. It is a beautiful walk up there that must have been most inspiring for the writer. Today you can take a cable car as an alternative. It was opened in 1890 and is running ever since without one accident. It starts in the Altstadt at Kornmarkt station. Up on Molkenkur you have to change over to the original old cable car. The view down to the city is breathtaking as the surprise that waits for you halfway, if you look up to the mountain. You should take the opportunity to walk back down to the city using the old "Himmelsleiter"-path ("Stairways to heaven"), which Twain used. It was actually up on the Königstuhl that he wrote chapter 16 of "Huckleberry Finn", as you will learn later in the book. Timetables for the cable cars vary between summer and winter, check by calling 22796.

There is a tower on top of Königstuhl from where you can see the city, Mannheim, Schwetzingen, the Odenwald and the Rhine Valley (on clear days you can almost see France in the west). The other tower is a relay station and is used as a communication facility by the U.S. Army. It is rumored by some locals to be one of the most important strategic military places in Europe.

30 or 40 little school girls at the Wirthschaft to-day when I left, all drinking beer at the tables in the open air. What at an atrocious sight to the total abstinent eye! *(1)*

Heidelberg hack fares very high – < same price as illuminating the castle – a > ½ mark a minute. From town to castle, 10 minutes, 3.50 – back, 5 minutes, 3.50. To Königsstuhl & back, 15 M. I can walk it in less than 1 ½ h.

Livy – 200 years ago Heiᵍ had a something which we have lost this beautiful Castle, but they lacked something which we have, a noble & pathetic ruin to contemplate & muse over. (A natural thought)

I – no, they visited ruins which had been peopled 500 yrs before – & these had ruins to visit. Find one stone of a ruin 1000 yrs old – even *they* had ruins to muse over. *(1)*

SOME OLD STATISTICS. In 1878 a telegram to New York cost 3.45 Mark a word. In Heidelberg twentyone breweries tried to meet the demand of beer drinkers, while three drugstores sold pharmaceuticals, including opium, which was much in use by American and German ladies of that time.

A student had to pay between 50 and 140 Marks a semester for a room while heating was another 25 Marks. A cup of coffee cost 10 to 20 Pfennigs, one beer 20 Pfennigs and a dinner from 60 Pfennigs upwards.

THE CASTLE

Heidelberg Castle must have been very beautiful before the French battered and bruised and scorched it two hundred years ago. The stone is brown with a pinkish tint and does not seem to stain easily. The dainty and elaborate ornamentation upon its two chief fronts is as delicately carved as if it had been intended for the interior of a drawing-room rather than for the outside of a house. Many fruit and flower clusters, human heads and grim projecting lions' heads are still as perfect in every detail as if they were new. But the statues which are ranked between the windows have suffered. These are life-size statues of old-time emperors, electors and similar grandees, clad in mail and bearing ponderous swords. Some have lost an arm, some a head, and one poor fellow is chopped off at the middle. There is a saying that if a stranger will pass over the drawbridge and walk across the court to the castle front without saying anything, he can make a wish and it will be fulfilled. But they say that the truth of this thing has never had a chance to be proved, for the reason that before any stranger can walk from the drawbridge to the appointed place the beauty of the palace front will extort an exclamation of delight from him.

A ruin must be rightly situated to be effective. This one could not have been better placed. It stands upon a commanding elevation, it is buried in green woods, there is no level ground about it, but, on the contrary, there are wooded terraces upon terraces, and one looks down through shining leaves into profound chasms and abysses where twilight reigns and the sun cannot intrude. Nature knows how to garnish a ruin to get the best effect. One of these old towers is split down the middle and one half has tumbled aside. It tumbled in such a way as to establish itself in a picturesque attitude. Then all it lacked was a fitting drapery, and Nature has furnished that. She has robed the rugged mass in flowers and verdure and made it a charm to the eye. The standing half exposes its arched and cavernous rooms to you like open, toothless mouths. There, too, the vines and flowers have done their work of grace. The rear portion of the tower has not been neglected either but is clothed with a clinging garment of polished ivy which hides the wounds and stains of time. Even the top is not left bare but is crowned with a flourishing group of trees and shrubs. Misfortune has done for this old tower what it has done for the human character sometimes – improved it.

A gentleman remarked one day that it might have been fine to live in the castle in the day of its prime but that we had one advantage which its vanished inhabitants lacked – the advantage of having a charming ruin to visit and muse over. But that was a hasty idea. Those people had the advantage of *us*. They had the fine castle to live in and they could cross the Rhine valley and muse over the stately ruin of Trifels besides. The Trifels people in their day, five hundred years ago, could go and muse over majestic ruins which have vanished, now, to the last stone. There have always been ruins, no doubt, and there have always been pensive people to sigh over them, and asses to scratch upon them their names and the important date of their visit. Within a hundred years after Adam left Eden the guide probably gave the usual general flourish with his hand and said: "Place where the animals were named, ladies and gentlemen. Place where the tree of the forbidden fruit stood. Exact spot where Adam and Eve first met. And here, ladies and gentlemen, adorned and hallowed by the names and addresses of three generations of tourists, we have the crumbling remains of Cain's altar – fine old ruin!" Then, no doubt, he taxed them a shekel apiece and let them go.

An illumination of Heidelberg Castle is one of the sights of Europe. The Castle's picturesque shape, its commanding situation midway up the steep and wooded mountainside, its vast size – these features combine to make an illumination a most effective spectacle. It is necessarily an expensive show and consequently rather infrequent. Therefore whenever one of these exhibitions is to take place the news goes about in the papers and Heidelberg is sure to be full of people on that night. I and my agent had one of these opportunities and improved it.

About half past seven on the appointed evening we crossed the lower bridge with some American students in a pouring rain and started up the road which borders the Neuenheim side of the river. This roadway was densely packed with carriages and foot-passengers, the former of all ages and the latter of all ages and both sexes. This black and solid mass was struggling painfully onward through the slop, the darkness and the deluge. We waded along for three-quarters of a mile and finally took up a position in an unsheltered beer-garden directly opposite the Castle. We could not *see* the Castle – or anything else, for that matter – but we could dimly discern the outlines of the mountain over the way through the pervading blackness and knew whereabouts the Castle was located. We stood on one of the hundred benches in the garden, under our umbrellas. The other ninety-nine were occupied by standing men and women, and they also had umbrellas. All the region round about and up and down the river-road was a dense wilderness of humanity hidden under an unbroken pavement of carriage tops and umbrellas. Thus we stood during two drenching hours. No rain fell on my head but the converging whalebone points of a dozen neighboring umbrellas poured little cooling streams of water down my neck and sometimes into my ears and thus kept me from getting hot and impatient. I had the rheumatism, too, and had heard that this was good for it. Afterward, however, I was led to believe that the water treatment is *not* good for rheumatism. There were even little girls in that dreadful place. A man held one in his arms just in front of me for as much as an hour, with umbrella-drippings soaking into her clothing all the time.

Spectacular fireworks, similar to the one Twain describes in his notes, still happen several times a year. Call Tourist Information for details, tel. 21341.

In the circumstances two hours was a good while for us to have to wait but when the illumination did at last come we felt repaid. It came unexpectedly, of course – things always do that have been long looked and longed for. With a perfectly breath-taking suddenness several vast sheaves of varicolored rockets were vomited skyward out of the black throats of the castle towers, accompanied by a thundering crash of sound, and instantly every detail of the prodigious ruin stood revealed against the mountainside and glowing with an almost intolerable splendor of fire and color. For some little time the whole building was a blinding crimson mass, the towers continued to spout thick columns of rockets aloft, and overhead the sky was radiant with arrowy bolts which clove their way to the zenith, paused, curved gracefully downward, then burst into brilliant fountain-sprays of richly colored sparks. The red fires died slowly down within the Castle and presently the shell grew nearly black outside. The angry glare that shone out through the broken arches and innumerable sashless windows now reproduced the aspect which the Castle must have borne in the old time when the French spoilers saw the monster bonfire which they had made there fading and smoldering toward extinction.

While we still gazed and enjoyed, the ruin was suddenly enveloped in rolling and rumbling volumes of vaporous green fire, then in dazzling purple ones. Then a mixture of many colors followed and drowned the great fabric in its blended splendors. Meantime the nearest bridge had been illuminated, and from several rafts anchored in the river, meteor showers of rockets, Roman candles, bombs, serpents and Catharine wheels were being discharged in wasteful profusion into the sky – a marvelous sight indeed to a person as little used to such spectacles as I was. For a while the whole region about us seemed as bright as day and yet the rain was falling in torrents all the time. The evening's entertainment presently closed and we joined the innumerable caravan of half-drowned spectators and waded home again.

The Castle grounds are very ample and very beautiful, and as they joined the Hotel grounds, with no fences to climb but only some nobly shaded stone stairways to descend, we spent a part of nearly every day in idling through their smooth walks and leafy groves. There was an attractive spot among the trees where were a great many wooden tables and benches, and there one could sit in the shade and pretend to sip at his foamy beaker of beer while he inspected the crowd. I say pretend because I only pretended to sip, without really sipping. That is the polite way. But when you are ready to go you empty the beaker at a draught. There was a brass band and it furnished excellent music every afternoon. Sometimes so many people came that every seat was occupied, every table filled. And never a rough in the assemblage – all nicely dressed fathers and mothers, young gentlemen and ladies and children, and plenty of university students and glittering officers, with here and there a gray professor or a peaceful old lady with her knitting, and always a sprinkling of gawky foreigners. Everybody had his glass of beer before him or his cup of coffee or his bottle of wine or his hot cutlet and potatoes. Young ladies chatted, or fanned themselves, or wrought at their crocheting or embroidering. The students fed sugars to their dogs or discussed duels or illustrated new fencing tricks with their little canes. And everywhere was comfort and enjoyment and everywhere peace and good-will to men. The trees were jubilant with birds and the paths with rollicking children. One could have a seat in that place and plenty of music any afternoon for about eight cents, or a family ticket for the season for two dollars.

For a change, when you wanted one, you could stroll to the Castle and burrow among its dungeons or climb about its ruined towers or visit its interior shows – the great Heidelberg Tun, for instance. Everybody has heard of the great Heidelberg Tun and most people have seen it, no doubt. It is a wine-cask as big as a cottage, and some traditions say it holds eighteen hundred thousand bottles, and other traditions say it holds eighteen hundred million barrels. I think it likely that one of these statements is a mistake and the other one a lie. However, the mere matter of capacity is a thing of no sort of consequence, since

The castle yard in 1878. Today it is still open to the public. During the summer classical concerts are played here regularly and once in a while a performance of "The Student Prince" can be seen.

the cask is empty, and indeed has always been empty, history says. An empty cask the size of a cathedral could excite but little emotion in me. I do not see any wisdom in building a monster cask to hoard up emptiness in it, when you can get a better quality, outside, any day, free of expense. What could this cask have been built for? The more one studies over that the more uncertain and unhappy he becomes. Some historians say that thirty couples, some say thirty thousand couples, can dance on the head of this cask at the same time. Even this does not seem to me to account for the building of it. It does not even throw light on it. A profound and scholarly Englishman – a specialist – who had made the great Heidelberg Tun his sole study for fifteen years told me he had at last satisfied himself that the ancients built it to make German cream in. He said that the average German cow yielded from one to two and a half teaspoonfuls of milk when she was not worked in the plow or the haywagon more than eighteen or nineteen hours a day. This milk was very sweet and good and of a beautiful transparent bluish tint. But in order to get cream from it in the most economical way a peculiar process was necessary. Now he believed that the habit of the ancients was to collect several milkings in a teacup, our it into the Great Tun, fill up with water and then skim off the cream from time to time as the needs of the German Empire demanded.

This began to look reasonable. It certainly began to account for the German cream which I had encountered and marveled over in so many hotels and restaurants. But a thought struck me –

"Why did not each ancient dairyman take his own teacup of milk and his own cask of water and mix them, without making a government matter of it?"

"Where could he get a cask large enough to contain the right proportion of water?"

Very true. It was plain that the Englishman had studied the matter from all sides. Still I thought I might catch him on one point, so I asked him why the modern empire did not make the nation's cream in the Heidelberg Tun instead of leaving it to rot away unused. But he answered as one prepared –

"A patient and diligent examination of the modern German cream has satisfied me that they do not use the Great Tun now because they have got a *bigger* one hid away somewhere. Either that is the case or they empty the spring milkings into the mountain torrents and then skim the Rhine all summer."

There is a museum of antiquities in the Castle, and among its most treasured relics are ancient manuscripts connected with German history. There are hundreds of these, and their dates stretch back through many centuries. One of them is a decree signed and sealed by the hand of a successor of Charlemagne in the year 896. A signature made by a hand which vanished out of this life near a thousand years ago is a more impressive thing than even a ruined castle. Luther's wedding-ring was shown me, also a fork belonging to a time anterior to our era, and an early bootjack. And there was a plaster cast of the head of a man who was assassinated about sixty years ago. The stab-wounds in the face were duplicated with unpleasant fidelity. One or two real hairs still remained sticking in the eyebrows of the cast. That trifle seemed to almost change the counterfeit into a corpse.

There are many aged portraits – some valuable, some worthless, some of great interest, some of none at all. I bought a couple – one a gorgeous duke of the olden time, and the other a comely blue-eyed damsel, a princess, maybe. I bought them to start a portrait-gallery of my ancestors with. I paid a dollar and a half for the duke and two and a half for the princess. One can lay in ancestors at even cheaper rates than these in Europe if he will mouse among old picture shops and look out for chances.

The "Altertums Museum" is gone today, but another famous collection took its place, the "Apothecary Museum". It is filled with ancient drugs and alchemistic tools and documents. You can find it on the ground floor of the castle building on the right. Tel. 25880.

STUDENT LIFE

The summer semester was in full tide; consequently the most frequent figure in and about Heidelberg was the student. Most of the students were Germans, of course, but the representatives of foreign lands were very numerous. They hailed from every corner of the globe, – for instruction is cheap in Heidelberg, and so is living, too. The Anglo-American Club, composed of British and American students, had twenty-five members, and there was still much material left to draw from.

Nine-tenths of the Heidelberg students wore no badge or uniform; the other tenth wore caps of various colors, and belonged to social organizations called "corps." There were five corps, each with a color of its own; there were white caps, blue caps, and red, yellow, and green ones. The famous duelfighting is confined to the "corps" boys. The *"kneip"* seems to be a specialty of theirs, too. Kneips are held, now and then, to celebrate great occasions, like the election of a beer king, for instance. The solemnity is simple; the five corps assemble at night, and at a signal they all fall loading themselves with beer, out of pint-mugs, as fast as possible, and each man keeps his own count, – usually by laying aside a lucifer match for each mug he empties. The election is soon decided. When the candidates can hold no more, a count is instituted and the one who has drank the greatest number of pints is proclaimed king. I was told that the last beer king elected by the corps, – or by his own capabilities, – emptied his mug seventy-five times. No stomach could hold all that quantity at one time, of course, – but there are ways of frequently creating a vacuum, which those who have been much at sea will understand.

One sees so many students abroad at all hours, that he presently begins to wonder if they ever have any working hours. Some of them have, some of them haven't. Each can choose for himself whether he will work or play; for German university life is a very free life; it seems to have no restraints. The student does not live in the college buildings, but hires his own lodgings, in any locality he prefers, and he takes his meals when and where he pleases. He goes to bed when it suits him, and does not get up at all unless he wants to. He is not entered at the university for any particular length of time; so he is likely to change about. He passes no examination upon entering college. He merely pays a trifling fee of five or ten dollars, receives a card entitling him to the privileges of the university, and that is the end of it. He is now ready for business, – or play, as he shall prefer. If he elects to work, he finds a large list of lectures to choose from. He selects the subjects which he will study, and enters his name for these studies; but he can skip attendance.

The result of this system is, that lecture-courses upon specialties of an unusual nature are often delivered to very slim audiences, while those upon more practical and every-day matters of education are delivered to very large ones. I heard of one case where, day after day, the lecturer's audience consisted of three students, – and always the same three. But one day two of them remained away. The lecturer began as usual, – "Gentlemen," – then, without a smile, he corrected himself, saying, – "Sir," – and went on with his discourse.

It is said that the vast majority of the Heidelberg students are hard workers, and make the most of their opportunities; that they have no surplus means to spend in dissipation, and no time to spare for frolicking. One lecture follows right on the heels of another, with very little time for the student to get out of one hall and into the next; but the industrious ones manage it by going on a trot. The professors assist them in the saving of their time by being promptly in their little boxed-up pulpits when the hours strike, and as promptly out again when the hour finishes. I entered an empty lecture-room one day just before the clock struck. The place had simple, unpainted pine desks and benches for about 200 persons.

About a minute before the clock struck, a hundred and fifty students swarmed in, rushed to their seats, immediately spread open their note-books and dipped their pens in the ink. When the clock began to strike, a burly professor entered, was received with a round of applause, moved swiftly down the center aisle, said "Gentlemen," and began to talk as he climbed his pulpit steps; and by the time he had arrived in his box and faced his audience, his lecture was well under way and all the pens were going. He had no notes, he talked with prodigious rapidity and energy for an hour, – then the students began to remind him in certain well understood ways that his time was up; he seized his hat, still talking, proceeded swiftly down his pulpit steps, got out the last word of his discourse as he struck the floor; everybody rose respectfully, and he swept rapidly down the aisle and disappeared. An instant rush for some other lecture room followed, and in a minute I was alone with the empty benches once more.

Yes, without doubt, idle students are not the rule. Out of eight hundred in the town, I knew the faces of only about fifty; but these I saw everywhere, and daily. They walked about the streets and the wooded hills, they drove in cabs, they boated on the river, they sipped beer and coffee, afternoons, in the Schloss gardens. A good many of them wore the colored caps of the corps. They were finely and fashionably dressed, their manners were quite superb, and they led an easy, careless, comfortable life. If a dozen of them sat together, and a lady or a gentleman passed whom one of them knew and saluted, they all rose to their feet and took off their caps. The members of a corps always received a fellow-member in this way, too; but they paid no attention to members of other corps; they did not seem to see them. This was not a discourtesy; it was only a part of the elaborate and rigid corps-etiquette.

There seems to be no chilly distance existing between the German students and the professor; but, on the contrary, a companionable intercourse, the opposite of chilliness and reserve. When the professor enters a beer hall in the evening where students are gathered together, these rise up and take off their caps, and invite the old gentleman to sit with them and partake. He accepts, and the pleasant talk and the beer flow for an hour or two, and by and by the professor, properly charged and comfortable, gives a cordial good night, while the students stand bowing and uncovered; and then he moves on his happy way homeward with all his vast cargo of learning afloat in his hold. Nobody finds fault or feels outraged; no harm has been done.

It seemed to be a part of corps-etiquette to keep a dog or so, too. I mean a corps-dog, – the common property of the organization, like the corps-steward or head servant; then there are other dogs, owned by individuals.

On a summer afternoon in the Castle gardens, I have seen six students march solemnly into the grounds, in single file, each carrying a bright Chinese parasol and leading a prodigious dog by a string. It was a very imposing spectacle. Sometimes there would be about as many dogs around the pavilion as

Founded in 1386, the University of Heidelberg is the most ancient university in Germany and one of the three oldest in Europe. In 1878 seventy professors were teaching 750 students – all of them men. The first womem students were admitted ten years later. Among the students were 33 Americans and 22 from Great Britain. Together they founded the Anglo-American Club. One of its first members was the famous writer Frank Harris.

Today about 28,000 students study here. The "new" University building on the south side of the Universitätsplatz in the heart of the Altstadt was built in 1930 with big financial help from the American ambassador in Berlin, Jacob Gould Schurman. He collected the sum of 500,000 US-Dollars among fellow German-Americans. He became a "honorable citizen" (Ehrenbürger) of the city and "Schurman-day" was celebrated on December 17th. Because some of the donators were Jews, the Nazis erased all signs of the donators in 1938. They took away the list of donators and replaced it with a bust of Adolf Hitler. The building was freed from the Nazis by the American army on March 31st, 1945.

Today you will find a new list of donators and a street running parallel with the Neckar river is named after Schurman.

students; and of all breeds and of all degrees of beauty and ugliness. These dogs had a rather dry time of it; for they were tied to the benches and had no amusement for an hour or two at a time except what they could get out of pawing at the gnats, or trying to sleep and not succeeding. However, they got a lump of sugar occasionally – they were fond of that.

It seemed right and proper that students should indulge in dogs; but everybody else had them, too, – old men and young ones, old women and nice young ladies. If there is one spectacle that is unpleasanter than another, it is that of an elegantly dressed young lady towing a dog by a string. It is said to be the sign and symbol of blighted love. It seems to me that some other way of advertising it might be devised, which would be just as conspicuous and yet not so trying to the proprieties.

It would be a mistake to suppose that the easy-going pleasure-seeking student carries an empty head. Just the contrary. He has spent nine years in the gymnasium, under a system which allowed him no freedom, but vigorously compelled him to work like a slave. Consequently, he has left the gymnasium with an education which is so extensive and complete, that the most a university can do for it is to perfect some of its profounder specialties. It is said that when a pupil leaves the gymnasium, he not only has a comprehensive education, but he *knows* what he knows, – it is not befogged with uncertainty, it is burnt into him so that it will stay. For instance, he does not merely read and write Greek, but speaks it; the same with the Latin. Foreign youth steer clear of the gymnasium; its rules are too severe. They go to the university to put a mansard roof on their whole general education; but the German student already has his mansard roof, so he goes there to add a steeple in the nature of some specialty, such as a particular branch of law, or medicine, or philology – like international law, or diseases of the eye, or special study of the ancient Gothic tongues. So this German attends only the lectures which belong to the chosen branch, and drinks his beer and tows his dog around and has a general good time the rest of the day. He has been in rigid bondage so long that the large liberty of university life is just what he needs and likes and thoroughly appreciates; and as it cannot last forever, he makes the most of it while it does last, and so lays up a good rest against the day that must see him put on the chains once more and enter the slavery of official or professional life.

THE STUDENT PRISON

I t seems that the student may break a good many of the public laws without having to answer to the public authorities. His case must come before the University for trial and punishment. If a policeman catches him in an unlawful act and proceeds to arrest him, the offender proclaims that he is a student, and perhaps shows his matriculation card, whereupon the officer asks for his address, then goes his way, and reports the matter at headquarters. If the offense is one over which the city has no jurisdiction, the authorities report the case officially to the University, and give themselves not further concern about it. The University court send for the student, listen to the evidence, and pronounce judgment. The punishment usually inflicted is imprisonment in the *University prison.*

As I understand it, a student's case is often tried without his being present at all. Then something like this happens: A constable in the service of the University visits the lodgings of the said student, knocks, is invited to come in, does so, and says politely –

"If you please, I am here to conduct you to prison."

"Ah," says the student, "I was not expecting it. What have I been doing?"

"Two weeks ago the public peace had the honor to be disturbed by you."

"It is true; I had forgotten it. Very well: I have been complained of, tried, and found guilty – is that it?"

"Exactly. You are sentenced to two days' solitary confinement in the College prison, and I am sent to fetch you."

Student. "O, I can't go to-day!"

Officer. "If you please – why?"

Student. "Because I've got an engagement."

Officer. "To-morrow, then, perhaps?"

Student. "No, I am going to the opera, to-morrow."

Officer. "Could you come Friday?"

Student (reflectively). "Let me see – Friday – Friday. I don't seem to have anything on hand Friday."

Officer. "Then, if you please, I will expect you on Friday."

Student. "All right, I'll come around Friday."

Officer. "Thank you. Good day, sir.

Student. "Good day."

So on Friday the student goes to the prison of his own accord, and is admitted.

It is questionable if the world's criminal history can show a custom more odd than this. Nobody knows, now, how it originated. There have always been many noblemen among the students, and it is presumed that all students are gentlemen; in the old times it was usual to mar the convenience of such folk as little as possible; perhaps this indulgent custom owes its origin to this.

One day I was listening to some conversation upon this subject when an American student said that for some time he had been under sentence for a slight breach of the peace and had promised the constable that he would presently find an unoccupied day and betake himself to prison. I asked the young gentleman to do me the kindness to go to jail as soon as he conveniently could, so that I might try to get in there and visit him, and see what college captivity was like. He said he would appoint the very first day he could spare.

The *Karzer* – or student prison – is located in the Augustinergasse, just behind the Old University, a few steps from the Universitätsplatz. Between 1778 and 1914 recalcitrant students were locked up here, leaving nothing but a graffiti behind. The Karzer is still open to the public Monday through Saturday, 9 am. till 6 pm., tel. 542334.

His confinement was to endure twenty-four hours. He shortly chose his day, and sent me word. I started immediately. When I reached the University Place, I saw two gentlemen talking together, and, as they had portfolios under their arms, I judged they were tutors or elderly students; so I asked them in English to show me the college jail. I had learned to take it for granted that anybody in Germany who knows anything, knows English, so I had stopped afflicting people with my German. These gentlemen seemed a trifle amused – and a trifle confused, too – but one of them said he would walk around the corner with me and show me the place. He asked me why I wanted to get in there, and I said to see a friend – and for curiosity. He doubted if I would be admitted, but volunteered to put in a word or two for me with the custodian.

He rang the bell, a door opened, and we stepped into a paved way and then into a small living-room, where we were received by a hearty and good-natured German woman of fifty. She threw up her hands with a surprised *"Ach Gott, Herr Professor!"* and exhibited a mighty deference for my new acquaintance. By the sparkle in her eye I judged she was a good deal amused, too. The "Herr Professor" talked to her in German, and I understood enough of it to know that he was bringing very plausible reasons to bear for admitting me. They were successful. So the Herr Professor received my earnest thanks and departed. The old dame got her keys, took me up two or three flights of stairs, unlocked a door, and we stood in the presence of the criminal. Then she went into a jolly and eager dexcription of all that had occurred downstairs, and what the Herr Professor had said, and so forth and so on. Plainly, she regarded it as quite a superior joke that I had waylaid a Professor and employed him in so odd a service. But I wouldn't have done it if I had known he was a Professor; therefore my conscience was not disturbed.

Now the dame left us to ourselves. The cell was not a roomy one; still it was a little larger than an ordinary prison cell. It had a window of good size, iron-gated; a small stove; two wooden chairs; two oaken tables, very old and most elaborately carved with names, mottoes, faces, armorial bearings, etc. – the work of several generations of imprisoned students; and a narrow wooden bedstead with a villainous old straw mattress, but no sheets, pillows, blankets, or coverlets – for these the student must furnish at his own cost if he wants them. There was no carpet, of course.

The ceiling was completely covered with names, dates, and monograms, done with candle-smoke. The walls were thickly covered with pictures and portraits (in profile), some done with ink, some with soot, some with a pencil, and some with red, blue, and green chalks; and wherever an inch or two of space had remained between the pictures, the captives had written plaintive

verses, or names and dates. I do not think I was ever in a more elaborately fres-
coed apartment.

Against the wall hung a placard containing the prison laws. I made a note of
one or two of these. For instance: The prisoner must pay, for the "privilege" of
entering, a sum equivalent to 20 cents of our money; for the privilege of leaving,
when his term has expired, 20 cents; for every day spent in the prison, 12 cents;
for fire and light, 12 cents a day. The jailer furnishes coffee, mornings, for a
small sum; dinners and suppers may be ordered from outside if the prisoner
chooses – and he is allowed to pay for them, too.

Here and there, on the walls, appeared the names of American students, and
in one place the American arms and motto were displayed in colored chalks.

With the help of my friend I translated many of the inscriptions. Some of
them were cheerful, others the reverse. I will give the reader a few specimens:

"In my tenth semester (my best one), I am cast here through the complaints
of others. Let those who follow me take warning."

"III Tage ohne Grund angeblich aus Neugierde." Which is to say, he had a
curiosity to know what prison life was like; so he made a breach in some law
and got three days for it. It is more than likely that he never had the same curiosity again.

(Transl.) "E. Glinicke, four days for being too eager a spectator of a row."

"F. Graf Bismarck – 27-29,II,'74." Which means that Count Bismarck, son
of the great statesman, was a prisoner two days in 1874.

(Transl.) "R. Diergandt – for Love – 4 days." Many people in this world
have caught it heavier than that for the same indiscretion.

This one is terse. I translate: "Four weeks for *misinterpreted gallantry.*"

I wish the sufferer had explained a little more fully. A four-weeks' term is
a rather serious matter.

There were many uncomplimentary references, on the walls, to a certain
unpopular college dignitary. One sufferer had got three days for not saluting
him. Another had "here two days slept and three nights lain awake," on account
of this same "Dr. K." In one place was a picture of Dr. K. hanging on a gallows.

Here and there, lonesome prisoners had eased the heavy time by altering the
records left by predecessors. Leaving the name standing, and the date and
length of the captivity, they had erased the description of the misdemeanor, and
written in its place, in staring capitals, "FOR THEFT!" or "FOR MURDER!" or
some other gaudy crime.

In one place, all by itself, stood this blood-curling word: "RACHE!" *

---

* *"Revenge!"*

There was no name signed, and no date. It was an inscription well calculated to pique curiosity. One would greatly like to know the nature of the wrong that had been done, and what sort of vengeance was wanted, and whether the prisoner ever achieved it or not. But there was no way of finding out these things.

Occasionally, a name was followed simply by the remark, "II days, for disturbing the peace," and without comment upon the justice or injustice of the sentence.

In one place was a hilarious picture of a student of the green cap corps with a bottle of champagne in each hand; and below was the legend: "These make an evil fate endurable."

There were two prison cells, and neither had space left on walls or ceiling for another name or portrait or picture. The inside surfaces of the two doors were completely covered with *cartes de visite* of former prisoners, ingeniously let into the wood and protected from dirt and injury by glass.

I very much wanted one of the sorry old tables which the prisoners had spent so many years in ornamenting with their pocket-knives, but red tape was in the way. The custodian could not sell one without an order from a superior; and that superior would have to get it from *his* superior; and that superior would have to get it from a higher one – and so on up and up until the faculty should sit on the matter and deliver final judgment. The system was right, and nobody could find fault with it; but it did not seem justifiable to bother so many people, so I proceeded no further. It might have cost me more than I could afford, anyway; for one of those prison tables, which was at that time in a private museum in Heidelberg, was afterward sold at auction for two hundred and fifty dollars. It was not worth more than a dollar, or possibly a dollar and a half, before the captive students began their work on it. Persons who saw it at the auction said it was so curiously and wonderfully carved that it was worth the money that was paid for it.

Among the many who have tasted the college prison's dreary hospitality was a lively young fellow from one of the Southern states of America, whose first year's experience of German university life was rather peculiar. The day he arrived in Heidelberg he enrolled his name on the college books, and was so elated with the fact that his dearest hope had found fruition and he was actually a student of the old and renowned university, that he set to work that very night to celebrate the event by a grand lark in company with some other students. In the course of his lark he managed to make a wide breach in one of the university's most stringent laws. Sequel: before noon, next day, he was in the college prison – booked for three months. The twelve long weeks dragged slowly by, and the day of deliverance came at last. A great crowd of sympathizing fellow-students received him with a rousing demonstration as he came forth, and of course there was another grand lark – in the course of which he managed to make a wide breach in one of the *city's* most stringent laws. Sequel: before noon, next day, he was safe in the city lockup – booked for three months. This second tedious captivity drew to an end in the course of time, and again a great crowd of sympathizing fellow-students gave him a rousing reception as he came forth; but his delight in his freedom was so boundless that he could not proceed soberly and calmly, but must go hopping and skipping and jumping down the sleety street from sheer excess of joy. Sequel: he slipped and broke his leg, and actually lay in the hospital during the next three months!

When he at last became a free man again, he said he believed he would hunt up a brisker seat of learning; the Heidelberg lectures might be good, but the opportunities of attending them were too rare, the educational process too slow; he said he had come to Europe with the idea that the acquirement of an education was only a matter of time, but if he had averaged the Heidelberg system correctly, it was rather a matter of eternity.

I have been gathering a lot of excellent matter here during the past ten days (stuff which has never been in a book) and shall finish gathering it in a week more (MTPL, p. 108). The "excellent matter" was evidently the college prison information. *(1)*

Laws. For every day spent in the Carcer, prisoner must pay 50 pf. For the priv. of entering, 90 pf. For privi. of going out, 90 pf.

Fire & light 50 pf per day.

You send out for your dinner & supper. The jailer furnishes coffee in morning some small price.

Dreadful old straw tick, no sheets or anything. But you are privileged to bring your own bedding.

Pine table with oaken top elaborately whittled with names, &c.

An oak table, ditto.

Two *hard* wood chairs. *(1)*

AT THE STUDENTS' DUELING GROUND

O ne day in the interest of science my agent obtained permission to bring me to the students' dueling place. We crossed the river and drove up the bank a few hundred yards, then turned to the left, entered a narrow alley, followed it a hundred yards and arrived at a two-story public house; we were acquainted with its outside aspect, for it was visible from the hotel. We went up stairs and passed into a large whitewashed apartment which was perhaps fifty feet long by thirty feet wide and twenty or twenty-five high. It was a well-lighted place. There was no carpet. Across one end and down both sides of the room extended a row of tables, and at these tables some fifty or seventy-five students were sitting.

Some of them were sipping wine, others were playing cards, others chess, other groups were chatting together, and many were smoking cigarettes while they waited for the coming duels. Nearly all of them wore colored caps; there were white caps, green caps, blue caps, red caps, and bright yellow ones; so, all the five corps were present in strong force. In the windows at the vacant end of the room stood six or eight long, narrow-bladed swords with large protecting guards for the hand, and outside was a man at work sharpening others on a

grindstone. He understood his business; for when a sword left his hand one could shave himself with it.

It was observable that the young gentlemen neither bowed to nor spoke with students whose caps differed in color from their own. This did not mean hostility, but only an armed neutrality. It was considered that a person could strike harder in the duel, and with a more earnest interest, if he had never been in a condition of comradeship with his antagonist; therefore, comradeship between the corps was not permitted. At intervals the presidents of the five corps have a cold official intercourse with each other, but nothing further. For example, when the regular dueling day of one of the corps approaches, its president calls for volunteers from among the membership to offer battle; three or more respond, – but there must not be less than three; the president lays their names before the other presiddents, with the request that they furnish antagonists for these challengers from among their corps. This is promptly done. It chanced that the present occasion was the battle day of the Red Cap Corps. They were the challengers, and certain caps of other colors had volunteered to meet them. The students fight duels in the room which I have described, *two days in every week during seven and a half or eight months in every year*. This custom has continued in Germany two hundred and fifty years.

To return to my narrative. A student in a white cap met us and introduced us to six or eight friends of his who also wore white caps, and while we stood conversing, two strange-looking figures were led in from another room. They were students panoplied for the duel. They were bareheaded; their eyes were protected by iron goggles which projected an inch or more, the leather straps of which bound their ears flat against their heads; their necks were wound around and around with thick wrappings which a sword could not cut through; from chin to ankle they were padded thoroughly against injury; their arms were bandaged and re-bandaged, layer upon layer, until they looked like solid black logs. These weird apparitions had been handsome youths, clad in fashionable attire, fifteen minutes before, but now they did not resemble any beings one ever sees unless in nightmares. They strode along, with their arms projecting straight out from their bodies; they did not hold them out themselves, but fellow students walked beside them and gave the needed support.

There was a rush for the vacant end of the room, now, and we followed and got good places. The combatants were placed face to face, each with several members of his own corps about him to assist; two seconds, well padded, and with swords in their hands, took near station; as a student belonging to neither of the opposing corps placed himself in a good position to umpire the combat; another student stood by with a watch and a memorandum-book to keep record of the time and the number and nature of the wounds; a gray-haired surgeon was present with his lint, his bandages, and his instruments. After a moment's pause the duelists saluted the umpire respectfully, then one after another the several officials stepped forward, gracefully removed their caps and saluted him also, and returned to their places. Everything was ready now; students stood crowded together in the foreground, and others stood behind them on chairs and tables. Every face was turned toward the center of attraction.

The combatants were watching each other with alert eyes; a perfect stillness, a breathless interest reigned. I felt that I was going to see some wary work. But not so. The instant the word was given, the two apparitions sprang forward and began to rain blows down upon each other with such lightning rapidity that I could not quite tell whether I saw the swords or only the flashes they made in the air; the rattling din of these blows, as they struck steel or paddings was something wonderfully stirring, and they were struck with such terrific force that I could not understand why the opposing sword was not beaten down under the assault. Presently, in the midst of the sword-flashes, I saw a handful of hair skip into the air as if it had lain loose on the victim's head and a breath of wind had puffed it suddenly away.

The seconds cried "Halt!" and knocked up the combatants' swords with their own. The duelists sat down; a student-official stepped forward, examined the wounded head and touched the place with a sponge once or twice; the surgeon came and turned back the hair from the wound – and revealed a crimson gash two or three inches long, and proceeded to bind an oval piece of leather and a bunch of lint over it; the tally keeper stepped up and tallied one for the opposition in his book.

Then the duelists took position again; a small stream of blood was flowing down the side of the injured man's head, and over his shoulder and down his body to the floor, but he did not seem to mind this. The word was given, and they plunged at each other as fiercely as before; once more the blows rained and rattled and flashed; every few moments the quick-eyed seconds would notice that a sword was bent – then they called "Halt!" struck up the contending weapons, and an assisting student straightened the bent one.

The wonderful turmoil went on – presently a bright spark sprung from a blade, and that blade, broken in several pieces, sent one of its fragments flying to the ceiling. A new sword was provided, and the fight proceeded. The exercise was tremendous, of course, and in time the fighters began to show great fatique. They were allowed to rest a moment, every little while; they got other rests by wounding each other, for then they could sit down while the doctor applied the lint and bandages. The law is that the battle must continue fifteen minutes if the men can hold out; and as the pauses do not count, this duel was protracted to twenty of thirty minutes, I judged. At last it was decided that the men were too much wearied to do battle longer. They were led away drenched with crimson from head to foot. That was a good fight, but it could not count, partly because it did not last the lawful fifteen minutes (of actual fighting), and partly because neither man was disabled by his wounds. It was a drawn battle, and corps law requires that drawn battles shall be re-fought as soon as the adversaries are well of their hurts.

During the conflict, I had talked a little, now and then, with a young gentleman of the White Cap corps, and he had mentioned that he was to fight next, – and had also pointed out his challenger, a young gentleman who was leaning against the opposite wall smoking a cigarette and restfully observing the duel then in progress.

My acquaintanceship with a party to the coming contest had the effect of giving me a kind of personal interest in it; I naturally wished he might win, and it was the reverse of pleasant to learn that he probably would not, because, although he was a notable swordsman, the challenger was held to be his superior.

The duel presently began and in the same furious way which had marked the previous one. I stood close by, but could not tell which blows told and which did not, they fell and vanished so like flashes of light. They all seemed to tell; the swords always bent over the opponents' heads, from the forehead back over the crown, and seemed to touch, all the way; but it was not so, – a protecting blade, invisible to me, was always interposed between. At the end of ten seconds each man had struck twelve or fifteen blows, and warded off twelve or fifteen, and no harm done; then a sword became disabled, and a short rest followed whilst a new one was brought. Early in the next round the white corps student got an ugly wound on the side of his head and gave his opponent one like it. In the third round the latter received another bad wound in the head, and the former had his under-lip divided. After that, the White Corps student gave many severe wounds, but got none of consequence in return. At the end of five minutes from the beginning of the duel the surgeon stopped it; the challenging party had suffered such injuries that any addition to them might be dangerous. These injuries were a fearful spectacle, but are better left undescribed. So, against expectation, my acquaintance was the victor.

The third duel was brief and bloody. The surgeon stopped it when he saw that one of the men had received such bad wounds that he could not fight longer without endangering his life.

"Apart from some obvious errors and misunderstandings, we have to admit that this description of a students' duel is exceptionally accurate and thrilling. A more just appreciation by a foreign writer is unlikely to be found." *(Deutsche Corpszeitung, 1898)*

"Das zweistöckige Wirtshaus" nowadays is a restaurant and hotel, called *Hotel Hirschgasse* (tel. 4032160). The original "Paukboden" still exists, but it is not open to the public. Here is a short chronological history provided by the hotel itself:

"In 1472, 20 years before the discovery of America, a short love story brought our 'Hirschgasse' to light for the first time in history. It was only in 1580, when Heidelberg's major, Heinrich Eckhardt, laid out a garden with a summer-house and fish ponds, that the inn 'Gasthaus zur Hirschgasse' was mentioned again. Subsequently, it sank into oblivion once more until the time when Georg Ditteney purchased the estate in 1791, and enlarged the inn by adding a major hall. Gangs of robbers terrorized the area and also held up the 'Hirschgasse'. When Ditteney discovered one of their lairs near the inn and reported it to the police, his life was in danger. Moreover, he shot a robber from the window sill and thus, for a long time, he slept behind barricaded windows with a loaded gun always close at hand. After 1800, times improved for the 'Hirschgasse'. Now the students' associations fought their duels in the hall of the 'Hirschgasse' and held their weekly carousals. In 1823, the proprietor's son started a thick dueling book which recalls the academic traditions of the former dueling house even to this day. The times of student duels and robbers are long gone. Today, visitors from all over the world meet at the 'Hotel Hirschgasse': yet the memories and history are ever present."

Up to 2,000 duels a year were fought and the beer consumption that went along with them was unbelievable. There are rumors of a student drinking 72 beers in one day. Even if the dueling was and still is illegal, this custom has survived, still takes place and is well and alive.

The anonoymous author of an article in the *Schwäb. Merkur* (November 24, 1935) pays tribute to two important living contemporaries of Mark Twain. The one is Paul Richards, the other the prototype of the German student who was immortalized by the humorist in *A Tramp Abroad*, the Prussian Landrat a. D. Herr von Flügge, from Speck, Kreis Naugard. Flügge studied in Heidelberg in 1878 and was a member of the "Korps Saxo-Borussia." Mark Twain became acquainted with him and described a *Mensur* in which Flügge participated. *(11)*

Students sent 2 to Berlin and 2 come here from Berlin, to fight.

This morning, 8 couples fought – 2 spectators fainted. One student had a piece of his scalp taken. The others' face so gashed up and floor all covered with blood. They only wear protecting spectacles.

Mr. Pfaff had a 6-inch piece of sword that had been broken in the fight. It was two edged and wonderfully whetted up and sharp.

They fight twice a week – in a Wirtschaft up a little road, opposite hotel on the other side of river.

Students with dreadfully scarred faces. Here you can't tell whether a man is a Franco-Prussian war hero, or merely had a university education. *(13)*

The forth duel was a tremendous encounter; but at the end of five or six minutes the surgeon interfered once more: another man so severely hurt as to render it unsafe to add to his harms. I watched this engagement as I had watched the others, – with rapt interest and strong excitement, and with a shrink and a shudder for every blow that laid open a cheek or a forehead; and a conscious paling of my face when I occasionally saw a wound of a yet more shocking nature inflicted. My eyes were upon the loser of this duel when he got his last and vanquishing wound, – it was in his face and it carried away his – but no matter, I must not enter into details. I had but a glance, and then turned quickly away, but I would not have been looking at all if I had known what was coming. No, that is probably not true; one thinks he would not look if he knew what was coming, but the interest and the excitement are so powerful that they would doubtless conquer all other feelings; and so, under the fierce exhilaration of the clashing steel, he would yield and look, after all. Sometimes spectators of these duels faint, – and it does seem a very reasonable thing to do, too.

Both parties to this fourth duel were badly hurt; so much so that the surgeon was at work upon them nearly or quite an hour, – a fact which is suggestive. But this waiting interval was not wasted in idleness by the assembled students. It was past noon; therefore they ordered their landlord, down stairs, to send up hot beefsteaks, chicken, and such things, and these they ate, sitting comfortably at the several tables, whilst they chatted, disputed and laughed. The door to the surgeon's room stood open, meantime, but the cutting, sewing, splicing, and bandaging going on in there in plain view did not seem to disturb anyone's appetite. I went in and saw the surgeon labor awhile, but could not enjoy it; it was much less trying to see the wounds given and received than to see them mended; the stir and turmoil, and the music of the steel, were wanting here, – one's nerves were wrung by this grisly spectacle, whilst the duel's compensating pleasurable thrill was lacking.

Finally the doctor finished, and the men who were to fight the closing battle of the day came forth. A good many dinners were not completed, yet, but no matter, they could be eaten cold, after the battle; therefore everybody crowded forward to see. This was not a love duel, but a "satisfaction" affair. These two students had quarreled, and were here to settle it. They did not belong to any of the corps, but they were furnished with weapons and armor, and permitted to fight here by the five corps as a courtesy. Evidently these two young men were unfamiliar with the dueling ceremonies, though they were not unfamiliar with the sword. When they were placed in position they thought it was time to begin, – and they did begin, too, and with a most impetuous energy, without waiting for anybody to give the word. This vastly amused the spectators, and even broke down their studied and courtly gravity and surprised them into laughter. Of course the seconds struck up the swords and started the duel over again. At the word, the deluge of blows began, but before long the surgeon once more interfered, – for the only reason which ever permits him to interfere, – and the day's war was over. It was now two in the afternoon, and I had been present since half past nine in the morning. The field of battle was indeed a red one by this time; but some sawdust soon righted that. There had been one duel before I arrived. In it one of the men received many injuries, while the other one escaped without a scratch.

I had seen the heads and faces of ten youths gashed in every direction by the keen two-edged blades, and yet had not seen a victim wince, nor heard a moan, or detected any fleeting expression which confessed the sharp pain the hurts were inflicting. This was good fortitude, indeed. Such endurance is to be expected in savages and prize fighters, for they are born and educated to it; but to find it in such perfection in these gently-bred and kindly-natured young fellows is matter for surprise. It was not merely under the excitement of the sword-play that this fortitude was shown; it was shown in the surgeon's room where an uninspiring quiet reigned, and where there was no audience. The doctor's manipulations brought out neither grimaces nor moans. And in the fights it was observable that these lads hacked and slashed with the same tremendous spirit, after they were covered with streaming wounds, which they had shown in the beginning.

The world in general looks upon the college duels as very farcial affairs: true, but considering that the college duel is fought by boys; that the swords are real swords; and that the head and face are exposed, it seems to me that it is a farce which has quite a grave side to it. People laugh at it mainly because they think the student is so covered up with armor that he cannot be hurt. But it is not so; his eyes and ears are protected, but the rest of his face and head are bare. He cannot only be badly wounded, but his life is in danger; and he would sometimes lose it but for the interference of the surgeon. It is not intended that his life shall be endangered. Fatal accidents are possible, however. For instance, the student's sword may break, and the end of it fly up behind his antagonist's ear and cut an artery which could not be reached if the sword remained whole. This has happened, sometimes, and death has resulted on the spot. Formerly the student's armpits were not protected, – and at that time the swords were pointed, whereas they are blunt, now; so an artery in the armpit was sometimes cut, and death followed. Then in the days of sharp-pointed swords, a spectator was an occasional victim, – the end of a broken sword flew five or ten feet and buried itself in his neck or his heart, and death ensued instantly. The student duels in Germany occasion two or three deaths every year, now, but this arises only from the carelessness of the wounded men; they eat or drink imprudently, or commit excesses in the way of overexertion; inflammation sets in and gets such a headway that it cannot be arrested. Indeed, there is blood and pain and danger enough about the college duel to entitle it to a considerable degree of respect.

All the customs, all the laws, all the details, pertaining to the student duel are quaint and naïve. The grave, precise, and courtly ceremony with which the thing is conducted, invests it with a sort of antique charm.

This dignity, and these knightly graces suggest the tournament, not the prize fight. The laws are as curious as they are strict. For instance, the duelist may step forward from the line he is placed upon, if he chooses, but never back of it. If he steps back of it, or even leans back, it is considered that he did it to avoid a blow or contrive an advantage; so he is dismissed from his corps in disgrace. It would seem but natural to step from under a descending sword unconsciously, and against one's will and intent, – yet this unconsciousness is not allowed. Again: if under the sudden anguish of a wound the receiver of it makes a grimace, he falls some degrees in the estimation of his fellows; his corps are ashamed of him: they call him "hare foot," which is the German equivalent for chicken-hearted.

In addition to the corps laws, there are some corps-usages which have the force of laws.

Perhaps the president of a corps notices that one of the membership who is no longer an exempt, – that is a freshman, – has remained a sophomore some little time without volunteering to fight; some day, the president, instead of calling for volunteers, will *appoint* this sophomore to measure swords with a student of another corps; he is free to decline – everybody says so, – there is no compulsion. This is all true, – but I have not heard of any student who *did* decline. He would naturally rather retire from the corps than decline; to decline, and still remain in the corps would make him unpleasantly conspicuous, and properly so, since he knew, when he joined, that his main business, as a member, would be to fight. No, there is no law against declining, – except the law of custom, which is confessedly stronger than written law, everywhere.

The ten men whose duels I had witnessed did not go away when their hurts were dressed, as I had supposed they would, but came back, one after another, as soon as they were free of the surgeon, and mingled with the assemblage in the dueling room. The white-cap student who won the second fight witnessed the remaining three, and talked with us during the intermissions. He could not talk very well, because his opponent's sword had cut his under lip in two, and then the surgeon had sewed it together and overlaid it with a profusion of white plaister patches; neither could he eat easily, still he contrived to accomplish a slow and troublesome luncheon while the last duel was preparing. The man who was the worst hurt of all played chess while waiting to see this engagement. A good part of his face was covered with patches and bandages, and all the rest of his head was covered and concealed by them. It is said that the student likes to appear on the street and in other public places in this kind of array, and that this predilection often keeps him out when exposure to rain or sun is a positive danger for him. Newly bandaged students are a very common spectacle in the public gardens of Heidelberg. It is also said that the student is glad to get wounds in the face, because the scars they leave will show so well there; and it is also said that these face wounds are so prized that youths have even been known to pull them apart from time to time and put red wine in them to make them heal badly and leave as ugly a scar as possible. It does not look reasonable, but it is roundly asserted and maintained, nevertheless; I am sure of one thing, – scars are plenty enough in Germany, among the young men; and very grim ones they are, too. They criss-cross the face in angry red welts, and are permanent and ineffaceable. Some of these scars are of a very strange and dreadful aspect; and the effect is striking when several such accent the milder ones, which form a city map on a man's face; they suggest the "burned district" then. We had often noticed that many of the students wore a colored silk band or ribbon diagonally across their breasts. It transpired that this signifies that the wearer has fought three duels in which a decision was reached – duels in which he either whipped or was whipped – for drawn battles do not count.* After a student had received his ribbon, he is "free"; he can cease from fighting, without reproach, – except some one insult him; his president cannot appoint him to fight; he can volunteer if he wants to, or remain quiescent if he prefers to do so. Statistics show that he does *not* prefer to remain quiescent. They show that the duel has a singular fascination about it somewhere, for these free men, so far from resting upon the privilege of the badge, are always volunteering.

---

* *FROM MY DIARY. – Dined in a hotel a few miles up the Neckar, in a room whose walls were hung all over with framed portrait-groups of the Five Corps; some were recent, but many antedated photography, and were pictured in lithography – the dates ranged back to forty or fifty years ago. Nearly every individual wore the ribbon across his breast. In one portrait-group representing (as each of these pictures did) an entire Corps, I took pains to count the ribbons: there were twenty-seven members, and twenty-one of them wore that significant badge.*

There was a student in Heidelberg who had picked up somewhere and mastered a peculiar trick of cutting up under instead of cleaving down from above. While the trick lasted he won in sixteen successive duels in his own university; but by that time observers had discovered what his charm was, and how to break it, therefore his championship ceased.

The rule which forbids social intercourse between members of different corps is strict. In the dueling house, in the parks, on the street, and anywhere and everywhere that students go, caps of a color group themselves together. If all the tables in a public garden were crowded but one, and that one had two red-cap students at it and ten vacant places, the yellow caps, and the green caps, seeking seats, would go by that table and not seem to see it, nor seem to be aware that there was such a table in the grounds. The student by whose courtesy we had been enabled to visit the dueling place, wore the white cap, – Prussian Corps. He introduced us to many white caps but to none of another color. The corps etiquette extended even to us, who where strangers, and required us to group with the white corps only, and speak only with the white corps, while we were their guests, and keep aloof from caps of the other colors. Once I wished to examine some of the swords, but an American student said, "It would not be quite polite; these now in the windos all have red hilts or blue; they will bring in some with white hilts presently, and those you can handle freely." When a sword was broken in the first duel, I wanted a piece of it; but its hilt was the wrong color, so it was considered best and politest to await a properer season. It was brought to me after the room was cleared, and I will now make a "life-size" sketch of it by tracing a line around it with my pen, to show the width of the weapon. The length of these swords is about three feet, and they are quite heavy. One's disposition to cheer, during the course of the duels or at their close, was naturally strong, but corps etiquette forbade any demonstrations of this sort. However brilliant a contest or a victory might be,

I thoroughly disapprove of duels. I consider them unwise, and I know they are dangerous. Still, I have always taken a great interest in other people's duels. One always feel an abiding interest in any heroic thing which has entered into his own experience.

In 1878, fourteen years after my unmaterialized duel, Messieurs Fortu and Gambetta fought a duel which made heroes of both of them in France, and made them ridiculous throughout the rest of the world. I was living in Munich that fall and winter, and I was so interested in that duel that I wrote a long account of it, and it is in one of my books, somewhere – an account which had some inaccuracies in it, but as an exhibition of the *spirit* of that duel, I think it was correct and trustworthy. *(8)*

no sign or sound betrayed that any one was moved. A dignified gravity and repression were maintained at all times.

When the dueling was finished and we were ready to go, the gentlemen of the Prussian Corps to whom we had been introduced took off their caps in the courteous German way, and also shook hands; their brethren of the same order took off their caps and bowed, but without shaking hands; the gentlemen of the other corps treated us just as they would have treated white caps, – they fell apart, apparently unconsciously, and left us an unobstructed pathway, but did not seem to see us or know we were there. If we had gone thither the following week as guests of another corps, the white caps, without meaning any offense, would have observed the etiquette of their order and ignored our presence.

IN THE OPERA

O ne day we took the train and went down to Mannheim to see King Lear played in German. It was a mistake. We sat in our seats three whole hours and never understood anything but the thunder and lightning; and even that was reversed to suit German ideas, for the thunder came first and the lightning followed after.

The behavior of the audience was perfect. There were no rustlings, or whisperings, or other little disturbances; each act was listened to in silence, and the applauding was done after the curtain was down. The doors opened at half past four, the play began promptly at half past five, and within two minutes afterward all who were coming were in their seats, and quiet reigned. A German gentleman in the train had said that a Shakespearian play was an appreciated treat in Germany and that we should find the house filled. It was true; all the six tiers were filled, and remained so to the end, – which suggested that it is not only balcony people who like Shakespeare in Germany, but those of the pit and the gallery, too.

Another time, we went to Mannheim and attended a shivaree, – otherwise an opera, – the one called Lohengrin. The banging and slamming and booming and crashing were something beyond belief. The racking and pitiless pain of it remains stored up in my memory alongside the memory of the time that I had my teeth fixed. There were circumstances which made it necessary for me to stay through the four hours to the end, and I stayed; but the recollection of that long, dragging, relentless season of suffering is indestructible. To have to endure it in silence, and sitting still, made it all the harder. I was in a railed compartment with eight or ten strangers, of the two sexes, and this compelled repression; yet at times the pain was so exquisite that I could hardly keep the tears back. At those times, as the howlings and wailings and shriekings of the singers, and the ragings and roarings and explosions of the vast orchestra rose higher and higher, and wilder and wilder, and fiercer and fiercer, I could have cried if I had been alone. Those strangers would not have been surprised to see a man do such a thing who was being gradually skinned, but they would have marveled at it here, and made remarks about it no doubt, whereas there was nothing in the present case which was an advantage over being skinned. There was a wait of half an hour at the end of the first act, and I could have gone out and rested during that time, but I could not trust myself to do it, for I felt that

I should desert and stay out. There was another wait of half an hour toward nine o'clock, but I had no spirit left, and so had no desire but to be let alone.

I do not wish to suggest that the rest of the people there were like me, for, indeed, they were not. Whether it was that they naturally liked that noise, or whether it was that they had learned to like it by getting used to it, I did not at that time know; but they did like it, – this was plain enough. While it was going on they sat and looked as rapt and grateful as cats do when one strokes their backs; and whenever the curtain fell they rose to their feet, in one solid mighty multitude, and the air was snowed thick with waving handkerchiefs, and hurricanes of applause swept the place. This was not comprehensible to me. Of course, there were many people there who were not under compulsion to stay; yet the tiers were as full at the close as they had been at the beginning. This showed that the people liked it.

It was a curious sort of a play. In the matter of costumes and scenery it was fine and showy enough; but there was not much action. That is to say, there was not much really done, it was only talked about; and always violently. It was what one might call a narrative play. Everybody had a narrative and a grievance, and none were reasonable about it, but all in an offensive and ungovernable state. There was little of that sort of customary thing where the tenor and the soprano stand down by the footlights, warbling, with blended voices, and keep holding out their arms toward each other and drawing them back and spreading both hands over first one breast and then the other with a shake and a pressure, – no, it was every rioter for himself and no blending. Each sang his indictive narrative in turn, accompanied by the whole orchestra of sixty instruments, and when this had continued for some time, and one was hoping they might come to an understanding and modify the noise, a great chorus composed entirely of maniacs would suddenly break forth, and then during two minutes, and sometimes three, I lived over again all that I had suffered the time the orphan asylum burned down.

We only had one brief little season of heaven and heaven's sweet ecstasy and peace during all this long and diligent and acrimoniuos reproduction of the other place. This was while a gorgeous procession of people marched around and around, in the third act, and sang the Wedding Chorus. To my untutored ear that was music, – almost divine music. While my seared soul was steeped in the healing balm of those gracious sounds, it seemed to me that I could almost re-suffer the torments which had gone before, in order to be so healed again. There is where the deep ingenuity of the operatic idea is betrayed. It deals so largely in pain that its scattered delights are prodigiously augmented by the contrasts. A pretty air in an opera is prettier there than it could be anywhere

Our term "star." I have often wondered what could suggest it. I perceive, now. Here, in the programme you find, in the list of names & characters –

Lohengrin .... ·X·
<[---] & nothing more>
Then at bottom .... X Loh
Heinrich .... Herr Mödlinger.
Lohengrin X
<L> Elsa .... Fräulien Ottiker
Herzog Gottfried, ... 〃 Ullmicher
Friederich .... Herr Plank
Ortrud .... Frau Seubert.

———

 LOHENGRIN .... Herr ALBERT NIEMANN

Doors open at half past 4 p.m. Performance begins at half past 5. Perf^{ce} closes at 10 P.M.

Significant that on Monday, no seats left except the 6 M (highest price) for Opera next Thursday – all cheaper ones gone. Opera is not a fashion, but a passion & it isn't dependent upon the swells, but upon every body.

At Lear, the whole 6 tiers were pretty full – the 6th as full as any.

Only 4 or 5 ladies with hats on – some held them in lap.

No music at all after beginning of play.

Curtain always dropped with every change of scene.

It was down only 1 minute. Down 1 ½ to 3 minutes between acts.

Scenes were changed utterly without noise.

Applause only once in the midst of an act, though at the end of acts there was thrice applause & once the king was recalled & once twic recaled.

No lights except on the stage

No ushers.

Very quiet well behaved audienc

They rustled papers occasionally.

Lear's great speeches sounded mighty flat. (Quote one.)

Quote some ads from newspaper.

We were the last in – 5 or 10 m after play began.

5 balconies & a parquet. Excellent house though no celebrated actor. Gentleman in train said a Shaks play was a feast in G.

The thunder generally preceded the lightning last night at theatre, which was wrong. *(1)*

In midst of it John who had not moved or spoken from the beginning, but looked the picture of patient suffering, was asked how he was getting along. He said in a tremulous voice <tremulous with tears> that he had not had just such a good time since the time he had his teeth fixed.

I will say this much for Lohengrin on my own account: it accomplished for me what no circumstance or combination of circumstances has ever been able to do before, since I first saw the light of this world: it gave me the headache. *(1)*

The great theatre jammed – standing room all sold.

The bridal song very sweet & beautiful – not another strain in the whole Opera that was pretty except choruses & some of the instrumental parts. It's an "historical" Opera, so to speak. First one & then another "relates" either in a linked scream, long drawn out, or (male) in a succession of war-whoops, with appropriate action. There seems to be little of that where the tenor & the soprano, sweetly & appealingly warbling, alternately hold out their arms toward each other as if preparing to catch a flour-sack, & then <clasp them together & hitches up her left breast> impressively spread them, first over one breast & then over the other, & pour their souls out in a blended strain. No, it was every rioter for himself, & no blending to speak of. – I recognized nothing I had ever heard before, except the bridal song.

I have attended Operas whenever I could not help it, for fourteen years, now, & I am sure I know of no agony comparable to the listening to an un-familiar Opera. I am enchanted with the airs in Trovatore & other old operas which the hand organ & the music box have made entirely familiar to my ear – I am carried away with delighted enthusiasm when they are sung at the Opera – but O, how far between they are! & what long, arid heart-breaking & head-aching between-times expanses of that sort of intense but incoherent noise which so reminds me of the time the orphan asylum burned down.

It was well put on the stage, & very beautiful. *(1)*

else, I suppose, just as an honest man in politics shines more than he would elsewhere.

I have since found out that there is nothing the Germans like so much as an opera. They like it, not in a mild and moderate way, but with their whole hearts. This is a legitimate result of habit and education. Our nation will like the opera, too, by and by, no doubt. One in fifty of those who attend our operas likes it already, perhaps, but I think a good many of the other forty-nine go in order to learn to like it, and the rest in order to be able to talk knowingly about it. The latter usually hum the airs while they are being sung, so that their neigh-bors may perceive that they have been to operas before. The funerals of these do not occur often enough.

A gentle, old-maidish person and a sweet young girl of seventeen sat right in front of us that night at the Mannheim opera. These people talked, between the acts, and I understood them, though I understood nothing that was uttered on the distant stage. At first they were guarded in their talk, but after they had heard my agent and me conversing in English they dropped their reserve and I picked up many of their little confidences; no, I mean many of *her* little con-fidences, – meaning the elder party, – for the young girl only listened, and gave assenting nods, but never said a word. How pretty she was, and how sweet she was! I wished she would speak. But evidently she was absorbed in her own thoughts, her own young-girl dreams, and found a dearer pleasure in silence. But she was not dreaming sleepy dreams, – no, she was awake, alive, alert, she could not sit still a moment. She was an enchanting study. Her gown was of a soft white silky stuff that clung to her round young figure like a fish's skin, and it was rippled over with the gracefullest little fringy films of lace; she had deep, tender eyes, with long, curved lashes; and she had peachy cheeks, and a dimpled chin, and such a dear little dewy rosebud of a mouth; and she was so dove-like, so pure, and so gracious, so sweet and bewitching. For long hours I did mightily wish she would speak. And at last she did; the red lips parted, and out leaped her thought, – and with such a guileless and pretty enthusiasm, too: "Auntie, I just *know* I've got five hundred fleas on me!"

That was probably over the average. Yes, it must have been very much over the average. The average at that time in the Grand Duchy of Baden was forty-five to a young person (when alone), according to the official estimate of the home secretary for that year; the average for older people was shifty and in-determinable, for whenever a wholesome young girl came into the presence of her elders she immediately lowered their average and raised her own. She became a sort of contribution-box. This dear young thing in the theater had been sitting there unconsciously taking up a collection. Many a skinny old being in our neighborhood was the happier and the restfuller for her coming.

In that large audience, that night, there were eight very conspicuous people. These were ladies who had their hats or bonnets on. What a blessed thing it would be if a lady could make herself conspicuous in our theaters by wearing her hat. It is not usual in Europe to allow ladies and gentlemen to take bonnets, hats, overcoats, canes, or umbrellas into the auditorium, but in Mannheim this rule was not enforced because the audiences were largely made up of people from a distance, and among these were always a few timid ladies who were afraid that if they had to go into an anteroom to get their things when the play was over, they would miss their train. But the great mass of those who came from a distance always ran the risk and took the chances, preferring the loss of the train to a breach of good manners and the discomfort of being unpleasantly conspicuous during a stretch of three or four hours.

Three or four hours. That is a long time to sit in one place, whether one be conspicuous or not, yet some of Wagner's operas bang along for six whole hours on a stretch! But the people sit there and enjoy it all, and wish it would last longer. A German lady in Munich told me that a person could not like Wagner's music at first, but must go through the deliberate process of learning to like it, – then he would have his sure reward; for when he had learned to like it he would hunger for it and never be able to get enough of it. She said that six hours of Wagner was by no means too much. She said that this composer had made a complete revolution in music and was burying the old masters one by one. And she said that Wagner's operas differed from all others in one notable respect, and that was that they were not merely spotted with music here and there, but were *all* music, from the first strain to the last. This surprised me. I said I had attended one of his insurrections, and found hardly *any* music in it except the Wedding Chorus. She said Lohengrin was noisier than Wagner's other operas, but that if I would keep on going to see it I would find by and by that it was all music, and therefore would then enjoy it. I *could* have said, "But would you advise a person to deliberately practice having the toothache in the pit of his stomach for a couple of years in order that he might then come to enjoy it?" But I reserved that remark.

This lady was full of the praises of the head-tenor who had performed in a Wagner opera the night before, and went on to enlarge upon his old and prodigious fame, and how many honors had been lavished upon him by the princely houses of Germany. Here was another surprise. I had attended that very opera, in the person of my agent, and had made close and accurate observations. So I said:

"Why, madam, *my* experience warrants me in stating that that tenor's voice is not a voice at all, but only a shriek, – the shriek of a hyena."

"That is very true," she said; "he cannot sing now; but in other times he sang, yes, divinely! So whenever he comes now, you shall see, yes, that the theater will not hold the people. *Jawohl bei Gott!* his voice is *wunderschön* in that past time."

I said she was discovering to me a kindly trait in the Germans which was worth emulating. I said that over the water we were not quite so generous; that with us, when a singer had lost his voice and a jumper had lost his legs, these parties ceased to draw. I said I had been to the opera in Hanover, once, and in Mannheim once, and in Munich (through my authorized agent) once, and this large experience had nearly persuaded me that the Germans *preferred* singers who couldn't sing. This was not such a very extravagant speech, either, for that burly Mannheim tenor's praises had been the talk of all Heidelberg for a week before his performance took place, – yet his voice was like the distressing noise which a nail makes when you screech it across a window-pane. I said so to Heidelberg friends the next day, and they said, in the calmest and simplest way, that that was very true, but that in earlier times his voice *had* been wonderfully fine. And the tenor in Hanover was just another example of this sort. The

English-speaking German gentleman who went with me to the opera there was brimming with enthusiasm over that tenor. He said:

"*Ach Gott!* a great man! You shall see him. He is so celebrate in all Germany, – and he has a pension, yes, from the government. He not obliged to sing now, only twice every year; but if he not sing twice each year they take him his pension away."

Very well, we went. When the renowned old tenor appeared, I got a nudge and an excited whisper:

"Now you see him!"

But the "celebrate" was an astonishing disappointment to me. If he had been behind a screen I should have supposed they were performing a surgical operation on him. I looked at my friend, – to my great surprise he seemed intoxicated with pleasure, his eyes were dancing with eager delight. When the curtain at last fell, he burst into the stormiest applause, and kept it up, – as did the whole house, – until the afflictive tenor had come three times before the curtain to make his bow. While the glowing enthusiast was swabbing the perspiration from his face, I said:

"I don't mean the least harm, but really, now, do you think he can sing?"

"Him? *No! Gott im Himmel, aber,* how he has been able to sing twenty-five years ago?" [Then pensively.] "*Ach,* no, *now* he not sing any more, he only cry. When he think he sing, now, he not sing at all, no, he only make like a cat which is unwell."

Where and how did we get the idea that the Germans are a stolid, phlegmatic race? In truth, they are widely removed from that. They are warm-hearted, emotional, impulsive, enthusiastic, their tears come at the mildest touch, and it is not hard to move them to laughter. They are the very children of impulse. We are cold and self-contained, compared to the Germans. They hug and kiss and cry and shout and dance and sing; and where we use one loving, petting expression they pour out a score. Their language is full of endearing diminutives; nothing that they love escapes the application of a petting diminutive, – neither the house, nor the dog, nor the horse, nor the grandmother, nor any other creature, animate or inanimate.

In the theaters at Hanover, Hamburg, and Mannheim, they had a wise custom. The moment the curtain went up, the lights in the body of the house went down. The audience sat in the cool gloom of a deep twilight, which greatly enhanced the glowing splendors of the stage. It saved gas, too, and people were not sweated to death.

When I saw King Lear played, nobody was allowed to see a scene shifted; if there was nothing to be done but slide a forest out of the way and expose a temple beyond, one did not see that forest split itself in the mdidle and go shrieking away, with the accompanying disenchanting spectacle of the hands and heels of the impelling impulse, – no, the curtain was always dropped for an instant, – one heard not the least movement behind it, – but when it went up, the next instant, the forest was gone. Even when the stage was being entirely re-set, one heard no noise. During the whole time that King Lear was playing, the curtain was never down two minutes at any one time. The orchestra played until the curtain was ready to go up for the first time, then they departed for the evening. Where the stage-waits never reach two minutes there is no occasion for music. I had never seen this two-minute business between acts but once before, and that was when the "Shaughraun" was played at Wallack's.

I was at a concert in Munich one night, the people were streaming in, the clock-hand pointed to seven, the music struck up, and instantly all movement in the body of the house ceased, – nobody was standing, or walking up the aisles, or fumbling with a seat, the stream of incomers had suddenly dried up at its source. I listened undisturbed to a piece of music that was fifteen minutes long, – always expecting some tardy ticket-holders to come crowding past my knees, and being continuously and pleasantly disappointed, – but when the last note was struck, here came the stream again. You see, they had made those late comers wait in the comfortable waiting-parlor from the time the music had begun until it was ended.

It was the first time I had ever seen this sort of criminals denied the privilege of destroying the comfort of a house full of their betters. Some of these were pretty fine birds, but no matter, they had to tarry outside in the long parlor under the inspection of a double rank of liveried footmen and waiting-maids who supported the two walls with their backs and held the wraps and traps of their masters and mistresses on their arms.

We had no footmen to hold our things, and it was not permissible to take them into the concert room; but there were some men and women to take charge of them for us. They gave us checks for them and charged a fixed price, payable in advance, – five cents.

In Germany they always hear one thing at an opera which has never yet been heard in America, perhaps, – I mean the closing strain of a fine solo or duet. We always smash into it with an earthquake of applause. The result is that we rob ourselves of the sweetest part of the treat; we get the whisky, but we don't get the sugar in the bottom of the glass.

Our way of scattering applause along through an act seems to me to be better than the Mannheim way of saving it all up till the act is ended. I do not see how an actor can forget himself and portray hot passion before a cold still audience. I should think he would feel foolish. It is a pain to me to this day, to remember how that old German Lear raged and wept and howled around the stage, with never a response from that hushed house, never a single outburst till the act was ended. To me there was something unspeakably uncomfortable in the solemn dead silences that always followed this old person's tremendous outpourings of his feelings. I could not help putting myself in his place, – I thought I knew how sick and flat he felt during those silences, because I remembered a case which came under my observation once, and which, – but I will tell the incident:

One evening on board a Mississippi steamboat, a boy of ten years lay asleep in a berth, – a long, slim-legged boy, he was, encased in quite a short shirt; it was the first time he had ever made a trip on a steamboat, and so he was troubled, and scared, and had gone to bed with his head filled with impending snaggings, and explosions, and conflagrations, and sudden death. About ten o'clock some twenty ladies were sitting around about the ladies' saloon, quietly reading, sewing, embroidering, and so on, and among them sat a sweet, benignant old dame with round spectacles on her nose and her busy knitting-needles in her hands. Now all of a sudden, into the midst of this peaceful scene burst that slim-shanked boy in the brief shirt, wild-eyed, erect-haired, and shouting, "Fire, fire! *jump and run, the boat's afire and there ain't a minute to lose!*" All those ladies looked sweetly up and smiled, nobody stirred, the old lady pulled her spectacles down, looked over them, and said, gently:

"But you mustn't catch cold, child. Run and put on your breast-pin, and then come and tell us all about it."

It was a cruel chill to give to a poor little devil's gushing vehemence. He was expecting to be a sort of hero – the creator of a wild panic – and here everybody sat and smiled a mocking smile, and an old woman made fun of his bugbear. I turned and crept humbly away – for I was that boy – and never even cared to discover whether I had dreamed the fire or actually seen it.

I am told that in a German concert or opera, they hardly ever encore a song; that though they may be dying to hear it again, their good breeding usually preserves them against requiring the repetition.

Kings may encore; that is quite another matter; it delights everybody to see that the King is pleased; and as to the actor encored, his pride and gratification are simply boundless. Still, there are circumstances in which even a royal encore –

But it is better to illustrate. The King of Bavaria is a poet, and has a poet's eccentricities – with the advantage over all other poets of being able to gratify them, no matter what form they may take. He is fond of the opera, but not fond of sitting in the presence of an audience; therefore, it has sometimes occured, in Munich, that when an opera has been concluded and the players were getting off their paint and finery, a command has come to them to get their paint and finery on again. Presently the King would arrive, solitary and alone, and the players would begin at the beginning and do the entire opera over again with only that one individual in the vast solemn theater for audience. Once he took an odd freak into his head. High up and out of sight, over the prodigious stage of the court theater is a maze of interlacing water-pipes, so pierced that in case of fire, innumerable little thread-like streams of water can be caused to descend; and in case of need, this discharge can be augmented to a pouring flood. American managers might make a note of that. The King was sole audience. The opera proceeded, it was a piece with a storm in it; the mimic thunder began to mutter, the mimic wind began to wail and sough, and the mimic rain to patter. The King's interest rose higher and higher; it developed into enthusiasm. He cried out:

"It is good, very good, indeed! But I will have real rain! Turn on the water!"

The manager pleaded for a reversal of the command; said it would ruin the costly scenery and the splendid costumes, but the King cried:

"No matter, no matter, I will have real rain! Turn on the water!"

So the real rain was turned on and began to descend in gossamer lances to the mimic flower beds and gravel walks of the stage. The richly-dressed actresses and actors tripped about singing bravely and pretending not to mind it. The King was delighted, – his enthusiasm grew higher. He cried out:

"Bravo, bravo! More thunder! more lightning! turn on more rain!"

The thunder boomed, the lightning glared, the storm-winds raged, the deluge poured down. The mimic royalty on the stage, with their soaked satins clinging to their bodies, slopped around ankle deep in water, warbling their sweetest and best, the fiddlers under the eaves of the stage sawed away for dear life, with the cold overflow spouting down the backs of their necks, and the dry and happy King sat in his lofty box and wore his gloves to ribbons applauding.

"More yet!" cried the King; "more yet, – let loose all the thunder, turn on all the water! I will hang the man that raises an umbrella!"

When this most tremendous and effective storm that had ever been produced in any theater was at last over, the King's approbation was measureless. He cried:

"Magnificent, magnificent! *Encore!* Do it again!"

But the manager succeeded in persuading him to recall the encore, and said the company would feel sufficiently rewarded and complimented in the mere fact that the encore was desired by his Majesty, without fatiguing him with a repetition to gratify their own vanity.

During the remainder of the act the lucky performers were those whose parts required changes of dress; the others were a soaked, bedraggled, and uncomfortable lot, but in the last degree picturesque. The stage scenery was ruined, trap-doors were so swollen that they wouldn't work for a week afterward, the fine costumes were spoiled, and no end of minor damages were done by that remarkable storm.

It was a royal idea – that storm – and royally carried out. But observe the moderation of the King; he did not insist upon his encore. If he had been a gladsome, unreflecting American opera-audience, he probably would have had his storm repeated and repeated until he drowned all those people.

May 24, theater, Mannheim. King Lear – performance began at 6 sharp. Never understood a word – by and by a terrific and perfectly natural peal of thunder and vivid lightning. G. said. "Thank heaven it thunders in English anyway." Afterwards, at home, said, "Sad three hours – never understood a word but the thunder and lightning." *(13)*

Sunday Night, 11th. Huge crowd out to-night to hear the band play the Fremersberg. I suppose it is very low grade music – I know it *must* be low grade music – because it so delighted me, it so warmed me, moved me, stirred me, uplifted me, enraptured me that at times I could have cried & at others split my throat with shouting. The great crowd was another evidence that it was low grade music; for only the few are educated up to a point where high class music gives pleasure. I have never heard enough classic music to be able to enjoy it; & the simple truth is, I detest it. Not mildly, but with all my heart. To me an opera is the very climax & cap-stone of the absurd, the fantastic the unjustifiable. I hate the very name of opera – partly because of the nights of suffering I have endured in its presence, & partly because I want to love it and can't. I suppose one naturally hates the things he wants to love & can't. In America the opera is an affectation. The seeming love for [it] is a lie. Nine out of every ten of the males are bored by it, & 5 out of 10 women. Yet how they applaud, the ignorant liars! –

What a poor lot we human beings are, anyway. If base music gives me wings, why should I want any other? But I do. I want to like the higher music because the higher & better like it. But you see, I want to like it without taking the necessary trouble & giving the thing the necessary amount of time & attention. The natural suggestion is, to get into that upper tier, that dress circle, by a lie: we will *pretend* we like it. This lie, this pretense, gives to opera what support it has in America. *(1)*

From Bayreuth he wrote "At the Shrine of St. Wagner," one of the best descriptions of that great musical festival that has been put into words. He paid full tribute to the performance, also to the Wagner devotion, confessing its genuineness.

"This opera of 'Tristan und Isolde' last night broke the hearts of all witnesses who were of the faith, and I know of some, and have heard of many, who could not sleep after it, but cried the night away. I feel strongly out of place here. Sometimes I feel like the one sane person in the community of the mad; sometimes I feel like the one blind man where all others see; the one groping savage in the college of the learned, and always during service I feel like a heretic in heaven."

He tells how he really enjoyed two of the operas, and rejoiced in supposing that his musical regeneration was accomplished and perfected; but alas! he was informed by experts that those particular events were not real music at all. Then he says:

"Well, I ought to have recognized the sign – the old, sure sign that has never failed me in matters of art. Whenever I enjoy anything in art it means that it is mighty poor. The private knowledge of this fact has saved me from going to pieces with enthusiasm in front of many and many a chromo. However, my base instinct does bring me profit sometimes; I was the only man out of 3,200 who got his money back on those two operas.

"I wish I *could* give those sharp satires on European life which you mention, but of course a man can't write successful satire except he be in a calm, judicial good-humor; whereas I *hate* travel, and I *hate* hotels, and I *hate* the opera, and I *hate* the old masters. In truth I don't ever seem to be in a good enough humor with anything to satirize it. No, I want to stand up before it and curse it and foam at the mouth, or take a club and pound it to rags and pulp. I have got in two or three chapters about Wagner's operas, and managed to do it without showing temper, but the strain of another such effort would burst me. *(2)*

GOING TO HEIDELBERG ON A RAFT

When the landlord learned that I and my agents were artists, our party rose perceptibly in his esteem; we rose still higher when he learned that we were making a pedestrian tour of Europe.

He told us all about the Heidelberg road, and which were the best places to avoid and which the best ones to tarry at; he charged me less than cost for the things I broke in the night; he put up a fine luncheon for us and added to it a quantity of great light-green plums, the pleasantest fruit in Germany; he was so anxious to do us honor that he would not allow us to walk out of Heilbronn, but called up Götz von Berlichingen's horse and cab and made us ride.

I made a sketch of the turnout. It is not a Work, it is only what artists call a "study" – a thing to make a finished picture from. This sketch has several blemishes in it; for instance, the wagon is not traveling as fast as the horse is. This is wrong. Again, the person trying to get out of the way is too small; he is out of perspective, as we say. The two upper lines are not the horse's back, they are the reins; – there seems to be a wheel missing – this would be corrected

Leaving Heilbronn

I have made a pedestrian trip up the Neckar to Heilbronn, with muslin-wound hat, leathern leggings, sun-umbrella, alpenstock, &c – *by rail*, – with my agent, – I employ an agent on a salary, & he does the real work when any is to be done, though I appropriate his emotions to myself & do his marvelling for him – & in yesterday's chapter we have started back to Heidelberg on a raft, & are having a good time. The raft is mine, since I have chartered it, & I shall pick up useful passengers here & there to tell me the legends of the ruined castles, & other things – perhaps the Captain who brought the news of the Pitcairn revolution. *(1)*

in a finished Work, of course. That thing flying out behind is not a flag, it is a curtain. That other thing up there is the sun, but I didn't get enough distance on it. I do not remember, now, what that thing is that is in front of the man who is running, but I think it is a haystack or a woman. This study was exhibited in the Paris Salon of 1879, but did not take any medal; they do not give medals for studies.

We discharged the carriage at the bridge. The river was full of logs, – long, slender, barkless pine logs, – and we leaned on the rails of the bridge, and watched the men put them together into rafts. These rafts were of a shape and construction to suit the crookedness and extreme narrowness of the Neckar. They were from 50 to 100 yards long, and they gradually tapered from a 9-log breadth at their sterns, to a 3-log breadth at their bow-ends. The main part of the steering is done at the bow, with a pole; the 3-log breadth there furnishes room for only the steersman, for these little logs are not larger around than an average young lady's waist. The connections of the several sections of the raft are slack and pliant, so that the raft may be readily bent into any sort of curve required by the shape of the river.

The Neckar is in many places so narrow that a person can throw a dog across it, if he has one; when it is also sharply curved in such places, the rafts-man has to do some pretty nice snug piloting to make the turns. The river is not always allowed to spread over its whole bed – which is as much as 30, and sometimes 40 yards wide, – but is split into three equal bodies of water, by stone dikes which throw the main volume, depth, and current into the central one. In low water these neat narrow-edged dikes project four or five inches above the surface, like the comb of a submerged roof, but in high water they are overflowed. A hatful of rain makes high water in the Neckar, and a basketful produces an overflow.

There are dikes abreast the Schloss Hotel, and the current is violently swift at that point. I used to sit for hours in my glass cage, watching the long, narrow rafts slip along through the central channel, grazing the right-bank dike and aiming carefully for the middle arch of the stone bridge below; I watched them in this way, and lost all this time hoping to see one of them hit the bridge-pier and wreck itself sometime or other, but was always disappointed. One was smashed there one morning, but I had just stepped into my room a moment to light a pipe, so I lost it.

While I was looking down upon the rafts that morning in Heilbronn, the dare-devil spirit of adventure came suddenly upon me, and I said to my comrades:

"*I* am going to Heidelberg on a raft. Will you venture with me?"

Bird waiting for a Fish, a
Common Spectacle.
(Perspective of Bird not Correct.)

Raft coming down between stone Dikes.

Raft curving itself through
crooked piece of River (merely
a study not a finished
picture)

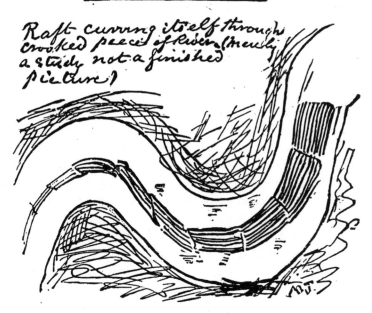

Their faces paled a little, but they assented with as good a grace as they could. Harris wanted to cable his mother, – thought it his duty to do that, as he was all she had in this world, – so, while he attended to this, I went down to the longest and finest raft and hailed the captain with a hearty "Ahoy, shipmate!" which put us upon pleasant terms at once, and we entered upon business. I said we were on a pedestrian tour to Heidelberg, and would like to take passage with him. I said this partly through young Z, who spoke German very well, and partly through Mr. X, who spoke it peculiarly. I can *understand* German as well as the maniac that invented it, but I *talk* it best through an interpreter.

The captain hitched up his trousers, then shifted his quid thoughtfully. Presently he said just what I was expecting he would say, – that he had no license to carry passengers, and therefore was afraid the law would be after him in case the matter got noised about or any accident happened. So I *chartered* the raft and the crew and took all the responsibilities on myself.

With a rattling song the starboard watch bent to their work and hove the cable short, then got the anchor home, and our bark moved off with a stately stride, and soon was bowling along at about two knots an hour.

Our party were grouped amidships. At first the talk was a little gloomy, and ran mainly upon the shortness of life, the uncertainty of it, the perils which beset it, and the need and wisdom of being always prepared for the worst; this shaded off into low-voiced references to the dangers of the deep, and kindred matters; but as the gray east began to redden and the mysterious solemnity and silence of the dawn to give place to the joy-songs of the birds, the talk took a cheerier tone, and our spirits began to rise steadily.

Germany, in the summer, is the perfection of the beautiful, but nobody has understood, and realized, and enjoyed the utmost possibilites of this soft and peaceful beauty unless he has voyaged down the Neckar on a raft. The motion of a raft is the needful motion; it is gentle, and gliding, and smooth, and noiseless; it calms down all feverish activities, it soothes to sleep all nervous hurry and impatience; under its restful influence all the troubles and vexations and sorrows that harass the mind vanish away, and existence becomes a dream, a charm, a deep and tranquil ecstasy. How it contrasts with hot and perspiring pedestrianism, and dusty and deafening railroad rush, and tedious jolting behind tired horses over blinding white roads!

We went slipping silently along, between the green and fragrant banks, with a sense of pleasure and contentment that grew, all the time. Sometimes the banks were overhung with thick masses of willows that wholly hid the ground behind; sometimes we had noble hills on one hand, clothed densely with foliage to their tops, and on the other hand open levels blazing with poppies, or clothed in the rich blue of the corn-flower; sometimes we drifted in the shadow of forests, and sometimes along the margin of long stretches of velvety grass, fresh and green and bright, a tireless charm to the eye. And the birds! – they were everywhere; they swept back and forth across the river constantly, and their jubilant music was never stilled.

It was a deep and satisfying pleasure to see the sun create the new morning, and gradually, patiently, lovingly, clothe it on with splendor after splendor, and glory after glory, till the miracle was complete. How different is this marvel observed from a raft, from what it is when one observes it through the dingy windows of a railway station in some wretched village while he munches a petrified sandwich and waits for the train.

DOWN THE RIVER

M en and women and cattle were at work in the dewy fields by this time. The people often stepped aboard the raft, as we glided along the grassy shores, and gossiped with us and with the crew for a hundred yards or so, then stepped ashore again, refreshed by the ride.

Only the men did this; the women were too busy. The women do all kinds of work on the continent. They dig, they hoe, they reap, they sow, they bear monstrous burdens on their backs, they shove similar ones long distances on wheelbarrows, they drag the cart when there is no dog or lean cow to drag it, – and when there is, they assist the dog or cow. Age is no matter, – the older the woman the stronger she is, apparently. On the farm a woman's duties are not defined, – she does a little of everything; but in the towns it is different, there she only does certain things, the men do the rest. For instance, a hotel chambermaid has nothing to do but make beds and fires in fifty or sixty rooms, bring towels and candles, and fetch several tons of water up several flights of stairs, a hundred pounds at a time, in prodigious metal pitchers. She does not have to work more than eighteen or twenty hours a day, and she can always get down on her knees and scrub the floors of halls and closets when she is tired and needs a rest.

As the morning advanced and the weather grew hot, we took off our outside clothing and sat in a row along the edge of the raft and enjoyed the scenery, with our sun umbrellas over our heads and our legs dangling in the water. Every now and then we plunged in and had a swim. Every projecting grassy cape had its joyous group of naked children, the boys to themselves and the girls to themselves, the latter usually in care of some motherly dame who sat in the shade of a tree with her knitting. The little boys swam out to us, sometimes, but the little maids stood knee deep in the water and stopped their splashing and frolicking to inspect the raft with their innocent eyes as it drifted by. Once we turned a corner suddenly and surprised a slender girl of twelve years or upward, just stepping into the water. She had not time to run, but she did what answered just as well; she promptly drew a lithe young willow bough athwart her white body with one hand, and then contemplated us with a simple and untroubled interest. Thus she stood while we glided by. She was a pretty creature, and she and her willow bough made a very pretty picture, and one which could not offend the modesty of the most fastidious spectator. Her white skin had a low bank of fresh green willows for background and effective contrast, – for she stood against them, – and above and out of them projected the eager faces and white shoulders of two smaller girls.

Toward noon we heard the inspiriting cry:

"Sail ho!"

"Where away?" shouted the captain.

"Three points off the weather bow!"

We ran forward to see the vessel. It proved to be a steamboat, – for they had begun to run a steamer up the Neckar, for the first time in May. She was a tug, and one of very peculiar build and aspect. I had often watched her from the hotel, and wondered how she propelled herself, for apparently she had no propeller or paddles. She came churning along, now, making a deal of noise of one kind and another, and aggravating it every now and then by blowing a hoarse whistle. She had nine keel-boats hitched on behind and following after her in a long, slender rank. We met her in a narrow place, between dikes, and there was hardly room for us both in the cramped passage. As she went grinding and groaning by, we perceived the secret of her moving impulse. She did not drive herself up the river with paddles or propeller, she pulled herself by hauling on a great chain. This chain is laid in the bed of the river and is only fastened at the two ends. It is seventy miles long. It comes in over the boat's bow, passes around a drum, and is payed out astern. She pulls on that chain, and so drags herself up the river or down it. She has neither bow nor stern, strictly speaking, for she has a long-bladed rudder on each end and she never turns around. She uses both rudders all the time, and they are powerful enough to enable her to turn to the right or the left and steer around curves, in spite of the strong resistance of the chain. I would not have believed that that impossible thing could be done; but I saw it done, and therefore I know that there is one impossible thing which *can* be done. What miracle will man attempt next?

We met many big keel-boats on their way up, using sails, mule power, and profanity – a tedious and laborious business. A wire rope led from the foretopmast to the file of mules on the tow-path a hundred yards ahead, and by dint of much banging and swearing and urging, the detachment of drivers managed to get a speed of two or three miles an hour out of the mules against the stiff current. The Neckar has always been used as a canal, and thus has given employment to a great many men and animals; but now that this steamboat is able, with a small crew and a bushel or so of coal, to take nine keel-boats farther up the river in one hour than thirty men and thirty mules can do it in two, it is believed that the old-fashioned towing industry is on its death-bed. A second steamboat began work in the Neckar three months after the first one was put in service.

At noon we stepped ashore and bought some bottled beer and got some chickens cooked, while the raft waited; then we immediately put to sea again, and had our dinner while the beer was cold and the chickens hot. There is no pleasanter place for such a meal than a raft that is gliding down the winding Neckar past green meadows and wooded hills, and slumbering villages, and craggy heights graced with crumbling towers and battlements.

In one place we saw a nicely dressed German gentleman without any spectacles. Before I could come to anchor he had got away. It was a great pity. I so wanted to make a sketch of him. The captain comforted me for my loss, however, by saying that the man was without any doubt a fraud who had spectacles, but kept them in his pocket in order to make himself conspicuous.

Below Hassmersheim we passed Hornberg, Götz von Berlichingen's old castle. It stands on a bold elevation 200 feet above the surface of the river; it has high vine-clad walls enclosing trees, and a peaked tower about 75 feet high. The steep hillside, from the castle clear down to the water's edge, is terraced, and clothed thick with grapevines. This is like farming a mansard roof. All the steeps along that part of the river which furnish the proper exposure, are given up to the grape. That region is a great producer of Rhine wines. The Germans are exceedingly fond of Rhine wines; they are put up in tall, slender bottles, and are considered a pleasant beverage. One tells them from vinegar by the label.

The Hornberg hill is to be tunneled, and the new railway will pass under the castle.

It seems that the heavy work in the quarries and the new railway gradings is done mainly by Italians. That was a revelation. We have the notion in our country that Italians never do heavy work at all, but confine themselves to the lighter arts, like organ-grinding, operatic singing, and assassination. We have blundered, that is plain.

All along the river, near every village, we saw little station houses for the future railway. They were finished and waiting for the rails and business. They were as trim and snug and pretty as they could be. They were always of brick or stone; they were of graceful shape, they had vines and flowers about them already, and around them the grass was bright and green, and showed that it was carefully looked after. They were a decoration to the beautiful landscape, not an offense. Wherever one saw a pile of gravel or a pile of broken stone, it was always heaped as trimly and exactly as a new grave or a stack of cannon-balls; nothing about those stations or along the railroad or the wagon road was

The "Kettenschleppschiffe" were, surprise, surprise, no subjects of Twain's wild imagination. They really did exist. It was 1878, on May 24th, that the 126 km long chain-ship-system from Mannheim to Heilbronn was opened. The big chain had exactly 1,909,091 parts, each 12 cm long. Its weight totalled 2,000 tons. The "Kettenschleppschiffahrt" ended in 1930 and was replaced by modern motor ships after locks were built in the river.

You can take a boat trip up the river to Neckarsteinach and even further during the warm season. The Neckar boat rides leave from below the convention hall ("Stadthalle"). Phone 20181 or 480064 for details.

Next to the "Weiße Flotte" (= white fleet) a ferry boat takes you across the river. For a few relaxing minutes you can leave the hectic bustle of the city behind and "sail" within a beautiful view of the castle, the Altstadt, Königstuhl (watch the cable cars!) and the river – up and downstream. Memories of Heidelberg are memories like this.

You can either take the boat right back or take a walk on the Neckarwiese to the Alte Brücke (old bridge). It only takes a few minutes, but it is worth doing, knowing that you are following Goethe's and other famous people's steps.

allowed to look shabby or be unornamental. The keeping a country in such beautiful order as Germany exhibits, has a wise practical side to it, too, for it keeps thousands of people in work and bread who would otherwise be idle and mischievous.

As the night shut down, the captain wanted to tie up, but I thought maybe we might make Hirschhorn, so we went on. Presently the sky became overcast, and the captain came aft looking uneasy. He cast his eye aloft, then shook his head, and said it was coming on to blow. My party wanted to land at once, – therefore I wanted to go on. The captain said we ought to shorten sail anyway, out of common prudence. Consequently, the larboard watch was ordered to lay in his pole. It grew quite dark, now, and the wind began to rise. It wailed through the swaying branches of the trees, and swept our decks in fitful gusts. Things were taking on an ugly look. The captain shouted to the steersman on the forward log:

"How's she heading?"

The answer came faint and hoarse from far forward:

"Nor'-east-and-by-nor', – east-by-east, half-east, sir."

"Let her go off a point!"

"Ay-aye, sir!"

"What water have you got?"

"Shoal, sir. Two foot large, on the stabbord, two and a half scant on the labboard!"

"Let her go off another point!"

"Ay-aye, sir!"

"Forward, men, all of you! Lively, now! Stand by to crowd her round the weather corner!"

"Ay-aye, sir!"

Then followed a wild running and trampling and hoarse shouting, but the forms of the men were lost in the darkness and the sounds were distorted and confused by the roaring of the wind through the shingle-bundles. By this time the sea was running inches high, and threatening every moment to engulf the frail bark. Now came the mate, hurrying aft, and said, close to the captain's ear, in a low, agitated voice:

"Prepare for the worst, sir, – we have sprung a leak!"

"Heavens! where?"

"Right aft the second row of logs."

"Nothing but a miracle can save us! Don't let the men know, or there will be a panic and mutiny! Lay her in shore and stand by to jump with the stern-line the moment she touches. Gentlemen, I must look to you to second my endeavors in this hour of peril. You have hats, – go forrard and bail for your lives!"

Down swept another mighty blast of wind, clothed in spray and thick darkness. At such a moment as this, came from away forward that most appalling of all cries that are ever heard at sea:

"*Man overboard!*"

The captain shouted:

"Hard a-port! Never mind the man! Let him climb aboard or wade ashore!"

Another cry came down the wind:

"Breakers ahead!"

"Where away?"

"Not a log's length off her port fore-foot!"

We had groped our slippery way forward, and were now bailing with the frenzy of despair, when we heard the mate's terrified cry, from far aft:

"Stop that dashed bailing, or we shall be aground!"

But this was immediately followed by the glad shout:

"Land aboard the starboard transom!"

"Saved!" cried the captain. "Jump ashore and take a turn around a tree and pass the bight aboard!"

The next moment we were all on shore weeping and embracing for joy, while the rain poured down in torrents. The captain said he had been a mariner for forty years on the Neckar, and in that time had seen storms to make a man's cheek blanch and his pulses stop, but he had never, never seen a storm that even approached this one. How familiar that sounded! For I have been at sea a good deal and have heard that remark from captains with a frequency accordingly.

We framed in our minds the usual resolution of thanks and admiration and gratitude, and took the first opportunity to vote it, and put it in writing and present it to the captain, with the customary speech.

We tramped through the darkness and the drenching summer rain full three miles, and reached "the Naturalist Tavern" in the village of Hirschhorn just an hour before midnight, almost exhausted from hardship, fatigue, and terror. I can never forget that night.

The landlord was rich, and therefore could afford to be crusty and disobliging; he did not at all like being turned out of his warm bed to open his house for us. But no matter, his household got up and cooked a quick supper for us, and we brewed a hot punch for ourselves, to keep off consumption. After supper and punch we had an hour's soothing smoke while we fought the naval battle over again and voted the resolutions; then we retired to exceedingly neat and pretty chambers up stairs that had clean, comfortable beds in them with heirloom pillow-cases most elaborately and tastefully embroidered by hand. Such rooms and beds and embroidered linen are as frequent in German village inns as they are rare in ours. Our villages are superior to German villages in more merits, excellences, conveniences, and privileges that I can enumerate, but the hotels do not belong in the list.

"The Naturalist Tavern" was not a meaningless name; for all the halls and all the rooms were lined with large glass cases which were filled with all sorts of birds and animals, glass-eyed, ably stuffed, and set up in the most natural and eloquent and dramatic attitudes. The moment we were abed, the rain cleared away and the moon came out. I dozed off to sleep while contemplating a great white stuffed owl which was lookingly intently down on me from a high perch with the air of a person who thought he had met me before, but could not make out for certain.

But young Z. did not get off so easily. He said that as he was sinking deliciously to sleep, the moon lifted away the shadows and developed a huge cat, on a bracket, dead and stuffed, but crouching, with every muscle tense, for a spring, and with its glittering glass eyes aimed straight at him. It made Z. uncomfortable. He tried closing his own eyes, but that did not answer, for a natural instinct kept making him open them again to see if the cat was still getting ready to launch at him, – which she always was. He tried turning his back, but that was a failure; he knew the sinister eyes were on him still. So at last he had to get up, after an hour or two of worry and experiment, and set the cat out in the hall. So he won, that time.

Twain had the U.S. Consul of Mannheim, Edward Smith, travelling with him. They took a boat to Hirschhorn, followed by a ride on a horse cart to Neckargemünd and then the train to Heidelberg. (Even though Twain's report tells us a different story.)

If you don't find the time for a boat trip up the river, don't miss going by car or train or bus to Neckargemünd, Neckarsteinach, Dilsberg, and Hirschhorn (where the famous Götz von Berlichingen lived for a while). You will enjoy great scenic views and castles all the way. Take the splendid walk from Neckarsteinach, the village of four castles, across the river and up the mountain to Dilsberg. The French tried to capture Dilsberg 300 years ago, but they didn't find a way into the guarded village. Make that walk and you'll see why!

"Hirschhorn church – hole under edge of old stone alter – make legend, hide hero in there & to sleep & feed – could come out at night & play ghost – no dogs allowed, else they would discover him."

Mark Twain abandoned the idea noted here, contenting himself in chapter 18 of *A Tramp Abroad* with the observation: "In the Chancel was a twisted stone column, and the captain told us a legend about it ... but I do not repeat his tale because there was nothing plausible about it except that the Hero wrenched this column into its present screw-shape with his hands, – just one single wrench." *(13)*

The stuffed great gray cat with staring, intelligent glass eyes, in the moonlight, that wouldn't let young Smith go to sleep (he was on the floor & it above on a bracket) till he got up & turned its head away. This at the Naturalists inn – every room & hall full of stuffed creatures, & the back yards full of odd living ones.

The rooms & bedding wonderfully nice, but the old man rich & indifferent. Trying to get his nephew from America to take the place & be his heir, but he won't. He is the boy in green-faced hunting coat who said "I'm an American!" & shook hands & sat down with us without further introduction. Nice boy.

In the garden fruit trees, which the boy knocked down for us; & odds & ends of ancient stone carvings damp & mildewed lying around, & then a swift stream literally alive with trout – but you can't fish there, because it belongs to Heidelberg & an individual rents it at $200 a year – & every fish in it is worth a dollar or thereabouts.

That poor raven all louse-eaten, & so humble & ashamed of his bare-sterned condition. He was Pathetic. *(1)*

Mark Twain, Twitchell-Harris and Edward Smith spent the night of August 9th 1878 at the "Hotel zum Naturalisten". It still exists today, having been rebuilt on the site of the original hotel in the seventies. One of their restaurants still is named after the famous American guest. Their phone number is 06272 / 2052.

HIRSCHHORN

In the morning we took breakfast in the garden, under the trees, in the delightful German summer fashion. The air was filled with the fragrance of flowers and wild animals; the living portion of the menagerie of the "Naturalist Tavern" was all about us. There were great cages populous with fluttering and chattering foreign birds, and other great cages and greater wire pens, populous with quadrupeds, both native and foreign. There were some free creatures, too, and quite sociable ones they were. White rabbits went loping about the place, and occasionally came and sniffed at our shoes and shins: a fawn, with a red ribbon on its neck, walked up and examined us fearlessly; rare breeds of chickens and doves begged for crumbs, and a poor old tailless raven hopped about with a humble, shame-faced mien which said, "Please do not notice my exposure, – think how you would feel in my circumstances, and be charitable." If he was observed too much, he would retire behind something and stay there until he judged the party's interest had found another object. I never have seen another dumb creature that was so morbidly sensitive. Bayard Taylor, who could interpret the dim reasonings of animals, and understood their moral natures better than most men, would have found some way to make this poor old chap forget his troubles for a while, but we had not his kindly art, and so had to leave the raven to his griefs.

After breakfast we climbed the hill and visited the ancient castle of Hirschhorn, and the ruined church near it. There were some curious old bas-reliefs leaning against the inner walls of the church, – sculptured lords of Hirschhorn in complete armor, and ladies of Hirschhorn in the picturesque court costumes of the Middle Ages. These things are suffering damage and passing to decay, for the last Hirschhorn has been dead two hundred years, and there is nobody now who cares to preserve the family relics. In the chancel was a twisted stone column, and the captain told us a legend about it, of course, for in the matter of legends he could not seem to restrain himself; but I do not repeat his tale because there was nothing plausible about it except that the Hero wrenched this column into its present screw-shape with his hands, – just one single wrench. All the rest of the legend was doubtful.

But Hirschhorn is best seen from a distance, down the river. Then the clustered brown towers perched on the green hilltop, and the old battlemented stone wall, stretching up and over the grassy ridge and disappearing in the leafy sea beyond, make a picture whose grace and beauty entirely satisfy the eye. We descended from the church by steep stone stairways which curved this way and that down narrow alleys between the packed and dirty tenements of the village. It was a quarter well stocked with deformed, leering, unkempt and uncombed idiots, who held out hands or caps and begged piteously. The people of the quarter were not all idiots, of course, but all that begged seemed to be, and were said to be.

I was thinking of going by skiff to the next town, Neckarsteinach; so I ran to the river side in advance of the party and asked a man there if he had a boat to hire. I suppose I must have spoken High-German, – Court German, – I intended it for that, anyway, – so he did not understand me. I turned and twisted my question around and about, trying to strike that man's average, but failed. He could not make out what I wanted. Now Mr. X. arrived, faced this same man, looked him in the eye, and emptied this sentence on him, in the most glib and confident way:

"Can man boat get here?"

The mariner promptly understood and promptly answered. I can comprehend why he was able to understand that particular sentence, because by mere accident all the words in it except "get" have the same sound and the same

It was actually near Hirschhorn where a group of native American Indians (among them some Hopi indians) stayed during their first "official" visit in Germany in 1973. They stayed for one week, holding speeches and performing dances in Heidelberg and sharing camp fires with native hippies and the well-known rock group Guru Guru. They had us translate all the names of local spots of importance, mountains and villages. Hirschhorn means: "The buck deer's horn"...

The exhibits Twain mentions are the collection of:

"Carl Langbein – The Naturalist. – Carl Langbein (1816-1881), patron and founder of the collection shown in the Tourist Centre (*Haus des Gastes*) was a descendant of a family of bakers and inn-keepers resident in Hirschhorn since the end of the 17th century. In 1858 he married Maria Götzen, also from Hirschhorn. This date also marks the beginning of his collection. Without concentrating on one particular area of interest Langbein gradually acquired an impressive number of works of art from various fields and different epochs, the greater part probably originating from Hirschhorn and the vicinity. Several hundred animals (mostly indigenous) stuffed and prepared by himself, molluscs and minerals complemented his 'collection of natural history and antiquities'. A special attraction, they formed part of the interior decoration of his inn. With an element of pride Langbein assumed the name of 'The Naturalist' and named his inn likewise ('*Zum Naturalisten*'). The present restaurant bearing that name, together with assembly rooms, was built in the site of the inn demolished in 1969. Langbein not only enjoyed an excellent reputation as a restaurateur, but also made himself a name through numerous other fields of activity: stimulated by his collection he studied local history, tried his hand at drawing, and proved a dexterous craftsman in the making and restoration of furniture.

Focal points within the collection: for visitors today the particular appeal of the Langbein Collection lies in its surprising variety, result of a way of collecting which is to be understood in the context of 19th century art and history. The following areas of interest are represented in the museum: Sculptures and architectural fragments (16th-19th century), paintings and prints (17th-19th century), arts and crafts exhibits (18th-19th century), religious and ethnic art (18th-19th century), furniture (16th-19th century), textile objects (18th-19th century), weapons, hunting gear and hunting trophies (18th-19th century), objects of everyday use (17th-19th century) as well as a comprehensive collection of coins and books. Of particular importance are certain volumes from the library of the former Carmelite monastery in Hirschhorn (e. g. a 14th century antiphonary) as well as parts of the interior remnants of the baroque high altar (1761-62), refectory furniture, fragments of a Renaissance tomb (1608).

The diorama consisting of some 180 stuffed animals which give an impressive survey of the indigenous fauna (in some cases of endangered animal species) is another important feature of the museum." *(from the Museum booklet)*

Today the whole collection is housed in the *"Langbein Museum"*, just down the road from the Hotel zum Naturalisten. Call them for information: 06272 / 1742.

meaning in German that they have in English; but how he managed to understand Mr. X.'s next remark puzzled me. I will insert it, presently. X. turned
away a moment, and I asked the mariner if he could not find a board, and so
construct an additional seat. I spoke in the purest German, but I might as well
have spoken in the purest Choctaw for all the good it did. The man tried his
best to understand me; he tried, and kept on trying, harder and harder, until I
saw it was really of no use, and said:

"There, don't strain yourself, – it is of no consequence."

Then X. turned to him and crisply said:

"Machen Sie a flat board."

I wish my epitaph may tell the truth about me if the man did not answer up
at once, and say he would go and borrow a board as soon as he had lit the pipe
which he was filling.

We changed our mind about taking a boat, so we did not have to go. I have
given Mr. X.'s two remarks just as he made them. Four of the five words in the
first one were English, and that they were also German was only accidental, not
intentional; three out of the five words in the second remark were English, and
English only, and the two German ones did not mean anything in particular, in
such a connection.

X. always spoke English, to Germans, but his plan was to turn the sentence
wrong end first and upside down, according to German construction, and
sprinkle in a German word without any essential meaning to it, here and there,
by way of flavor. Yet he always made himself understood. He could make those
dialect-speaking raftsmen understand him, sometimes, when even young Z. had
failed with them; and young Z. was a pretty good German scholar. For one
thing, X. always spoke with such confidence, – perhaps that helped. And possibly the raftsmen's dialect was what is called *platt-Deutsch,* and so they found
his English more familiar to their ears than another man's German. Quite indifferent students of German can read Fritz Reuter's charming platt-Deutsch
tales with some little facility because many of the words are English. I suppose
this is the tongue which our Saxon ancestors carried to England with them. By
and by I will inquire of some other philologist.

However, in the meantime it had transpired that the men employed to caulk
the raft had found that the leak was not a leak at all, but only a crack between
the logs, – a crack which belonged there, and was not dangerous, but had been
magnified into a leak by the disordered imagination of the mate. Therefore we
went aboard again with a good degree of confidence, and presently got to sea
without accident. As we swam smoothly along between the enchanting shores,
we fell to swapping notes about manners and customs in Germany and else-

where. As I write, now, many months later, I perceive that each of us, by observing and noting and inquiring, diligently and day by day, had managed to lay in a most varied and opulent stock of misinformation. But this is not surprising; it is very difficult to get accurate details in any country.

If one asks a German a civil question, he will be quite sure to get a civil answer. If you stop a German in the street and ask him to direct you to a certain place, he shows no sign of feeling offended. If the place be difficult to find, ten to one the man will drop his own matters and go with you and show you.

In London, too, many a time, strangers have walked several blocks with me to show me my way.

There is something very real about this sort of politeness. Quite often, in Germany, shopkeepers who could not furnish me the article I wanted have sent one of their employés with me to show me a place where it could be had.

DILSBERG

However, I wander from the raft. We made the port of Neckarsteinach in good season, and went to the hotel and ordered a trout dinner, the same to be ready against our return from a two-hour pedestrian excursion to the village and castle of Dilsberg, a mile distant, on the other side of the river. I do not mean that we proposed to be two hours making two miles, – no, we meant to employ most of the time in inspecting Dilsberg.

For Dilsberg is a quaint place. It is most quaintly and picturesquely situated, too. Imagine the beautiful river before you; then a few rods of brilliant green sward on its opposite shore; then a sudden hill, – no preparatory gently rising slopes, but a sort of instantaneous hill, – a hill two hundred and fifty or three hundred feet high, as round as a bowl, with the same taper upward that an inverted bowl has, and with about the same relation of height to diameter that distinguishes a bowl of good honest depth, – a hill which is thickly clothed with green bushes, – a comely, shapely hill, rising abruptly out of the dead level of the surrounding green plains, visible from a great distance down the bends of the river, and with just exactly room on the top of its head for its steepled and turreted and roof-clustered cap of architecture, which same is tightly jammed and compacted within the perfectly round hoop of the ancient village wall.

There is no house outside the wall on the whole hill, or any vestige of a former house; all the houses are inside the wall, but there isn't room for another one. It is really a finished town, and has been finished a very long time. There is no space between the wall and the first circle of buildings; no, the village wall is itself the rear wall of the first circle of buildings, and the roofs jut a little over the wall and thus furnish it with eaves. The general level of the massed roofs is gracefully broken and relieved by the dominating towers of the ruined castle and the tall spires of a couple of churches; so, from a distance Dilsberg has rather more the look of a king's crown than a cap. That lofty green eminence and its quaint coronet form quite a striking picture, you may be sure, in the flush of the evening sun.

We crossed over in a boat and began the ascent by a narrow, steep path which plunged us at once into the leafy deeps of the bushes. But they were not cool deeps by any means, for the sun's rays were weltering hot and there was little or no breeze to temper them. As we panted up the sharp ascent, we met brown, bareheaded and barefooted boys and girls, occasionally, and sometimes men; they came upon us without warning, they gave us good-day, flashed out of sight in the bushes, and were gone as suddenly and mysteriously as they had come. They were bound for the other side of the river to work. This path had been traveled by many generations of these people. They have always gone down to the valley to earn their bread, but they have always climbed their hill again to eat it, and to sleep in their snug town.

It is said that the Dilsbergers do not emigrate much; they find that living up there above the world, in their peaceful nest, is pleasanter than living down in the troublous world. The seven hundred inhabitants are all blood-kin to each other, too; they have always been blood-kin to each other for fifteen hundred years; they are simply one large family, and they like the home folks better than they like strangers, hence they persistently stay at home. It has been said that for ages Dilsberg has been merely a thriving and diligent idiot factory. I saw no idiots there, but the captain said, "Because of late years the government has taken to lugging them off to asylums and otherwheres; and government wants to cripple the factory, too, and is trying to get these Dilsbergers to marry out of the family, but they don't like to."

The captain probably imagined all this, as modern science denies that the intermarrying of relatives deteriorates the stock.

Arrived within the wall, we found the usual village sights and life. We moved along a narrow, crooked lane which had been paved in the Middle Ages. A strapping, ruddy girl was beating flax or some such stuff in a little bit of a goods-box of a barn, and she swung her flail with a will, – if it was a flail; I was not farmer enough to know what she was at; a frowsy, barelegged girl was herding half a dozen geese with a stick, – driving them along the lane and keeping them out of the dwellings; a cooper was at work in a shop which I know he did not make so large a thing as a hogshead in, for there was not room. In the front rooms of dwellings girls and women were cooking or spinning, and ducks and chickens were waddling in and out, over the threshold, picking up chance crumbs and holding pleasant converse; a very old and wrinkled man sat asleep before his door, with his chin upon his breast and his extinguished pipe in his lap; soiled children were playing in the dirt everywhere along the lane, unmindful of the sun.

Except the sleeping old man, everybody was at work, but the place was very still and peaceful, nevertheless; so still that the distant cackle of the successful hen smote upon the ear but little dulled by intervening sounds. That commonest of village sights was lacking here, – the public pump, with its great stone tank or trough of limpid water, and its group of gossiping pitcher-bearers; for there is no well or fountain or spring on this tall hill; cisterns of rain water are used.

Our alpenstocks and muslin tails compelled attention, and as we moved through the village we gathered a considerable procession of little boys and girls, and so went in some state to the castle. It proved to be an extensive pile of crumbling walls, arches, and towers, massive, properly grouped for picturesque effect, weedy, grass-grown, and satisfactory. The children acted as guides; they walked us along the top of the highest wall, then took us up into a high tower and showed us a wide and beautiful landscape, made up of wavy distances of woody hills, and a nearer prospect of undulating expanses of green lowlands, on the one hand, and castle-graced crags and ridges on the other, with the shining curves of the Neckar flowing between. But the principal show, the chief pride of the children, was the ancient and empty well in the grass-grown court of the castle. Its massive stone curb stands up three or four feet above ground, and is whole and uninjured. The children said that in the Middle Ages this well was four hundred feet deep, and furnished all the village with an abundant supply of water, in war and peace. They said that in that old day its bottom was below the level of the Neckar, hence the water supply was inexhaustible.

But there were some who believed it had never been a well at all, and was never deeper than it is now, – eighty feet; that at that depth a subterranean passage branched from it and descended gradually to a remote place in the

Way back in 1969, when the hippies were all over Heidelberg continuing the tradition of the old romantics von Brentano, Hölderlin and Achim von Arnim, I used to be among them. Taking a trip to the beautiful Dilsberg one day, my girlfriend and I decided to speak only english just for the fun of it. To our amazement, the locals took us for descendants of those people who had emigrated from Dilsberg to the States a long time ago. They were exited and very friendly and in the local grocery we didn't even have to pay. A very lovely place indeed!

"There are such precise details in the story of Twain, that we have to assume that he really did visit Dilsberg." *(Ortsvorsteher Stefan Wiltschko, Dilsberg, 1985)*

"The great humorist could not have guessed, that seventy years after his visit his American compatriots would take a Jeep or Chevrolet up to the top of Dilsberg..." *(Rhein Neckar Zeitung, Heidelberg, January 3rd, 1949)*

A young American boy, nephew of a German emigrant had read Twain's account of Dilsberg and its mysterious well. When he traveled to Germany in the early 20th century, he was still fascinated by that story. He went to Dilsberg and got so excited that he had himself let down on a rope into the well. He didn't find anything, but when he returned some years later as a wealthy person, he invested a great amount of money in having the well thoroughly explored. A tunnel was found and there is still a plate saying "This tunnel was found and reopened with the help of Fritz von Briesen, New York."

"I have asked the old people of Dilsberg about the legend that Mark Twain told of our village. Nobody has ever heard of it before." *(Stefan Wiltschko, 1985)*

In a letter to his friend Howell, dated Jan. 30th, Munich, Twain confessed that he made up this "nice little legend" for Dilsberg. "Maybe the only part of this book that I will make up."

The old Burglinde.
A whirlwind felled this tree in 1923.

valley, where it opened into somebody's cellar or other hidden recess, and that the secret of this locality is now lost. Those who hold this belief say that herein lies the explanation that Dilsberg, besieged by Tilly and many a soldier before him, was never taken; after the longest and closest sieges the besiegers were astonished to perceive that the besieged were as fat and hearty as ever, and as well furnished with munitions of war, – therefore it must be that the Dilsbergers had been bringing these things in through the subterranean passage all the time.

The children said that there was in truth a subterranean outlet down there, and they would prove it. So they set a great truss of straw on fire and threw it down the well, while we leaned on the curb and watched the glowing mass descend. It struck bottom and gradually burned out. No smoke came up. The children clapped their hands and said:

"You see! Nothing makes so much smoke as burning straw – now where did the smoke go to, if there is no subterranean outlet?"

So it seemed quite evident that the subterranean outlet indeed existed. But the finest thing within the ruin's limits was a noble linden, which the children said was four hundred years old, and no doubt it was. It had a mighty trunk and a mighty spread of limb and foliage. The limbs near the ground were nearly the thickness of a barrel.

That tree had witnessed the assaults of men in mail, – how remote such a time seems, and how ungraspable is the fact that real men ever did fight in real armor! – and it had seen the time when these broken arches and crumbling battlements were a trim and strong and stately fortress, fluttering its gay banners in the sun, and peopled with vigorous humanity, – how impossibly long ago that seems! – and here it stands yet, and possibly may still be standing here, sunning itself and dreaming its historical dreams, when to-day shall have been joined to the days called "ancient."

Well, we sat down under the tree to smoke, and the captain delivered himself of his legend:

THE LEGEND OF DILSBERG CASTLE

It was to this effect. In the old times there was once a great company assembled at the castle, and festivity ran high. Of course there was a haunted chamber in the castle, and one day the talk fell upon that. It was said that whoever slept in it would not wake again for fifty years. Now when a young knight named Conrad von Geisberg heard this, he said that if the castle were his he would destroy that chamber, so that no foolish person might have the chance to bring so dreadful a misfortune upon himself and afflict such as loved him with the memory of it. Straightway, the company privately laid their heads together to contrive some way to get this superstitious young man to sleep in that chamber.

And they succeeded – in this way. They persuaded his betrothed, a lovely mischievous young creature, niece of the lord of the castle, to help them in their plot. She presently took him aside and had speech with him. She used all her persuasions, but could not shake him; he said his belief was firm, that if he should sleep there he would wake no more for fity years, and it made him shudder to think of it. Catharina began to weep. This was a better argument; Conrad could not hold out against it. He yielded and said she should have her wish if she would only smile and be happy again. She flung her arms about his neck, and the kisses she gave him showed that her thankfulness and her pleasure were very real. Then she flew to tell the company her success, and the applause she received made her glad and proud she had undertaken her mission, since all alone she had accomplished what the multitude had failed in.

At midnight, that night, after the usual feasting, Conrad was taken to the haunted chamber and left there. He fell asleep, by and by.

When he awoke again and looked about him, his heart stood still with horror! The whole aspect of the chamber was changed. The walls were mouldy and hung with ancient cobwebs; the curtains and beddings were rotten; the furniture was rickety and ready to fall to pieces. He sprang out of the bed, but his quaking knees sunk under him and he fell to the floor.

"This is the weakness of age," he said.

He rose and sought his clothing. It was clothing no longer. The colors were gone, the garments gave way in many places while he was putting them on. He fled, shuddering, into the corridor, and along it to the great hall. Here he was met by a middle-aged stranger of a kind countenance, who stopped and gazed at him with surprise. Conrad said:

"Good sir, will you send hither the lord Ulrich?"

The stranger looked puzzled a moment, then said:

"The lord Ulrich?"

"Yes, – if you will be so good."

The stranger called, – "Wilhelm!" A young serving man came, and the stranger said to him:

"Is there a lord Ulrich among the guests?"

"I know none of the name, so please your honor."

Conrad said, hesitatingly:

"I did not mean a guest, but the lord of the castle, sir."

The stranger and the servant exchanged wondering glances. Then the former said:

"I am the lord of the castle."

"Since when, sir?"

"Since the death of my father, the good lord Ulrich, more than forty years ago."

Conrad sank upon a bench and covered his face with his hands while he rocked his body to and fro and moaned. The stranger said in a low voice to the servant:

"I fear me this poor old creature is mad. Call some one."

In a moment several people came, and grouped themselves about, talking in whispers. Conrad looked up and scanned the faces about him wistfully.

Then he shook his head and said, in a grieved voice:

"No, there is none among ye that I know. I am old and alone in the world. They are dead and gone these many years that cared for me. But sure, some of these aged ones I see about me can tell me some little word or two concerning them."

Several bent and tottering men and women came nearer and answered his questions about each former friend as he mentioned the names. This one they said had been dead ten years, that one twenty, another thirty. Each succeeding blow struck heavier and heavier. At last the sufferer said:

"There is one more, but I have not the courage to, – O my lost Catharina!"

One of the old dames said:

"Ah, I knew her well, poor soul. A misfortune overtook her lover, and she died of sorrow nearly fifty years ago. She lieth under the linden tree without the court."

Conrad bowed his head and said:

"Ah, why did I ever wake! And so she died of grief for me, poor child. So young, so sweet, so good! She never wittingly did a hurtful ding in all the little summer of her life. Her loving debt shall be repaid – for I will die of grief for her."

His head dropped upon his breast. In a moment there was a wild burst of joyous laughter, a pair of round young arms were flung about Conrad's neck and a sweet voice cried:

"There, Conrad mine, thy kind words kill me, – the farce shall go no further! Look up, and laugh with us, – 't was all a jest!"

As he did look up, and gazed, in a dazed wonderment, – for the disguises were stripped away, and the aged men and women were bright and young and gay again. Catharina's happy tongue ran on:

"'Twas a marvelous jest, and bravely carried out. They gave you a heavy sleeping draught before you went to bed, and in the night they bore you to a ruined chamber where all had fallen to decay, and placed these rags of clothing by you. And when your sleep was spent and you came forth, two strangers, well instructed in their parts, were here to meet you; and all we, your friends, in our disguises, were close at hand, to see and hear, you may be sure. Ah, 'twas a gallant jest! Come, now, and make thee ready for the pleasures of the day. How real was thy misery for the moment, thou poor lad! Look up and have thy laugh, now!"

He looked up, searched the merry faces about him in a dreamy way, then sighed and said:

"I am aweary, good strangers, I pray you lead me to her grave."

All the smile vanished away, every cheek blanched, Catharine sunk to the ground in a swoon.

All day the people went about the castle with troubled faces, and communed together in undertones. A painful hush pervaded the place which had lately been so full of cheery life. Each in his turn tried to arouse Conrad out of his hallucination and bring him to himself; but all the answer any got was a meek, bewildered stare, and then the words:

"Good stranger, I have no friends, all are at rest these many years; ye speak me fair, ye mean me well, but I know ye not; I am alone and forlorn in the world, – prithee lead me to her grave."

During two years Conrad spent his days, from the early morning till the night, under the linden tree, mourning over the imaginary grave of his Catharina. Catharina was the only company of the harmless madman. He was very friendly toward her because, as he said, in some ways she reminded him of his Catharina whom he had lost "fifty years ago." He often said:

"She was so gay, so happy-hearted, – but you never smile; and always when you think I am not looking, you cry."

When Conrad died, they buried him under the linden, according to his directions, so that he might rest "near his poor Catharina." Then Catharina sat under the linden alone, every day and all day long, a great many years, speaking to no one, and never smiling; and at last her long repentance was rewarded with death, and she was buried by Conrad's side.

Harris pleased the captain by saying it was a good legend; and pleased him further by adding:

"Now that I have seen this mighty tree, vigorous with its four hundred years, I feel a desire to believe the legend for *its* sake; so I will humor the desire, and consider that the tree really watches over those poor hearts and feels a sort of human tenderness for them."

We returned to Neckarsteinach, plunged our hot heads into the trough at the town pump, and then went to the hotel and ate our trout dinner in leisurely comfort, in the garden, with the beautiful Neckar flowing at our feet, the quaint Dilsberg looming beyond, and the graceful towers and battlements of a couple of medieval castles (called the "Swallow's Nest" and "The Brothers") assisting the rugged scenery of a bend of the river down to our right. We got to sea in season to make the eight-mile run to Heidelberg before the night shut down. We sailed by the hotel in the mellow glow of sunset, and came slashing down with the mad current into the narrow passage between the dikes. I believed I could shoot the bridge myself, so I went to the forward triplet of logs and relieved the pilot of his pole and his responsibility.

We went tearing along in a most exhilarating way, and I performed the delicate duties of my office very well indeed for a first attempt; but perceiving, presently, that I really was going to shoot the bridge itself instead of the archway under it, I judiciously stepped ashore. The next moment I had my long-coveted desire: I saw a raft wrecked. It hit the pier in the center and went all to smash and scatteration like a box of matches struck by lightning.

I was the only one of our party who saw this grand sight; the others were attitudinizing, for the benefit of the long rank of young ladies who were promenading on the bank, and so they lost it. But I helped to fish them out of the river, down below the bridge, and then described it to them as well as I could.

They were not interested, though. They said they were wet and felt ridiculous and did not care anything for descriptions of scenery. The young ladies, and other people, crowded around and showed a great deal of sympathy, but that did not help matters; for my friends said they did not want sympathy, they wanted a back alley and solitude.

THE AWFUL GERMAN LANGUAGE

The summer days passed pleasantly in Heidelberg. We had a skilled trainer, and under his instructions we were getting our legs in the right condition for the contemplated pedestrian tours. We were well satisfied with the progress which we had made in the German language and more than satisfied with what we had accomplished in art.

I went often to look at the collection of curiosities in Heidelberg Castle, and one day I surprised the keeper of it with my German. I spoke entirely in that language. He was greatly interested and after I had talked a while he said my German was very rare, possibly a "unique," and wanted to add it to his museum.

If he had known what it had cost me to acquire my art he would also have known that it would break any collector to buy it. Harris and I had been hard at work on our German during several weeks at that time, and although we had made good progress it had been accomplished under great difficulty and annoyance, for three of our teachers had died in the meantime. A person who has not studied German can form no idea of what a perplexing language it is.

Surely there is not another language that is so slipshod and systemless and so slippery and elusive to the grasp. One is washed about in it hither and thither in the most helpless way and when at last he thinks he has captured a rule which offers firm ground to take a rest on amid the general rage and turmoil of the ten parts of speech, he turns over the page and reads, "Let the pupil make careful note of the following *exceptions.*" He runs his eye down and finds that there are more exceptions to the rule than instances of it. So overboard he goes again to hunt for another Ararat and find another quicksand. Such has been and continues to be my experience. Every time I think I have got one of these four confusing "cases" where I am master of it, a seemingly insignificant preposition intrudes itself into my sentence, clothed with an awful and unsuspected power, and crumbles the ground from under me. For instance, my book inquires after a certain bird – (it is always inquiring after things which are of no sort of consequence to anybody): "Where is the bird?" Now the answer to this question – according to the gook – is that the bird is waiting in the blacksmith shop on account of the rain. Of course no bird would do that, but then you must stick to the book. Very well, I begin to cipher out the German for that answer. I begin at the wrong end, necessarily, for that is the German idea. I say to myself,

"*Regen* (rain) is masculine – or maybe it is feminine – or possibly neuter – it is too much trouble to look now. Therefore, it is either *der* (the) Regen, or *die* (the) Regen, or *das* (the) Regen, according to which gender it may turn out to be when I look. In the interest of science, I will cipher it out on the hypothesis that it is masculine. Very well – then *the* rain is *der* Regen, if it is simply in the quiescent state of being *mentioned*, without enlargement or discussion – Nominative case. But if this rain is lying around in a kind of a general way on the ground, it is then definitely located, it is *doing something* – that is, *resting* (which is one of the German grammar's ideas of doing something), and this throws the rain into the Dative case and makes it *dem* Regen. However, this rain is not resting but is doing something *actively* – it is falling – to interfere with the bird, likely – and this indicates *movement,* which has the effect of sliding it into the Accusative case and changing *dem* Regen into *den* Regen." Having completed the grammatical horoscope of this matter, I answer up confidently and state in German that the bird is staying in the blacksmith shop "wegen (on account of) *den* Regen." Then the teacher lets me softly down with the remark that whenever the word "wegen" drops into a sentence it *always* throws that subject into the *Genitive* case, regardless of consequences – and that therefore this bird stayed in the blacksmith shop "wegen *des* Regens."

N. B. – I was informed, later, by a higher authority, that there was an "exception" which permits one to say "wegen *den* Regen" in certain peculiar and complex circumstances but that this exception is not extended to do anything *but* rain.

There are ten parts of speech and they are all troublesome. An average sentence in a German newspaper is a sublime and impressive curiosity. It occupies a quarter of a column. It contains all the ten parts of speech – not in regular order but mixed. It is built mainly of compound words constructed by the writer on the spot and not to be found in any dictionary – six or seven words compacted into one, without joint or seam – that is, without hyphens. It treats of fourteen or fifteen different subjects, each inclosed in a parenthesis of its own, with here and there extra parentheses which reinclose three or four of the minor parentheses, making pens within pens. Finally, all the parentheses and reparentheses are massed together between a couple of king-parentheses, one of which is placed in the first line of it – *after which comes the* VERB, and you find out for the first time what the man has been talking about. And after the verb – merely by way of ornament, as far as I can make out – the writer shovels in *"haben sind gewesen gehabt haben geworden sein,"* or words to that effect, and the monument is finished. I suppose that this closing hurrah is in the nature of the flourish to a man's signature – not necessary, but pretty. German books are easy enough to read when you hold them before the looking-glass or stand on your head – so as to reverse the construction – but I think that to learn to read and understand a German newspaper is a thing which must always remain an impossibility to a foreigner.

Yet even the German books are not entirely free from attacks of the Parenthesis distemper – though they are usually so mild as to cover only a few lines, and therefore when you at last get down to the verb it carries some meaning to your mind because you are able to remember a good deal of what has gone before.

Now here is a sentence from a popular and excellent German novel – with a slight parenthesis in it. I will make a perfectly literal translation and throw in the parenthesis-marks and some hyphens for the assistance of the reader – though in the original there are no parentheses-marks or hyphens, and the reader is left to flounder through to the remote verb the best way he can:

"But when he, upon the street, the (in-satin-and-silk-covered-now-very-unconstrainedly-after-the-newest-fashion-dressed) government counselor's wife *met,*" etc., etc.*

That is from *The Old Mamselle's Secret,* by Mrs. Marlitt. And that sentence is constructed upon the most approved German model. You observe how far that verb is from the reader's base of operations. Well, in a German newspaper they put their verb away over on the next page and I have heard that sometimes after stringing along on exciting preliminaries and parentheses for a column or

---

* *Wenn er aber auf der Strasse der in Sammt und Seide gehüllten jetz sehr ungenirt nach der neusten mode gekleideten Regierungsrathin begegnet.*

two they get in a hurry and have to go to press without getting to the verb at all. Of course, then the reader is left in a very exhausted and ignorant state.

We have the Parenthesis disease in our literature too and one may see cases of it every day in our books and newspapers but with us it is the mark and sign of an unpractised writer or a cloudy intellect, whereas with the Germans it is doubtless the mark and sign of a practised pen and of the presence of that sort of luminous intellectual fog which stands for clearness among these people. For surely it is *not* clearness – it necessarily can't be clearness. Even a jury would have penetration enough to discover that. A writer's ideas must be a good deal confused, a good deal out of line and sequence, when he starts out to say that a man met a counselor's wife in the street, and then right in the midst of this so simple undertaking halts these approaching people and makes them stand still until he jots down an inventory of the woman's dress. That is manifestly absurd. It reminds a person of those dentists who secure your instant and breathless interest in a tooth by taking a grip on it with the forceps and then stand there and drawl through a tedious anecdote before they give the dreaded jerk. Parentheses in literature and dentistry are in bad taste.

The Germans have another kind of parenthesis, which they make by splitting the verb in two and putting half of it at the beginning of an exciting chapter and the *other half* at the end of it. Can any one conceive of anything more confusing than that? These things are called "separable verbs." The German grammar is blistered all over with separable verbs and the wider the two portions of one of them are spread apart the better the author of the crime is pleased with his performance. A favorite one is *reiste ab* – which means *departed.* Here is an example which I culled from a novel and reduced to English:

"The trunks being now ready, the DE · after kissing his mother and sisters, and once more pressing to his bosom his adored Gretchen, who, dressed in simple white muslin, with a single tuberose in the ample folds of her rich brown hair, had tottered feebly down the stairs, still pale from the terror and excitement of the past evening, but longing to lay her poor aching head yet once again upon the breast of him whom she loved more dearly than life itself, PARTED."

The German language became one of the interests of the Clemens home during the early months of 1878. The Clemenses had long looked forward to a sojourn in Europe, and the demand for another Mark Twain book of travel furnished an added reason for their going. They planned for the spring sailing, and to spend a year or more on the Continent, making their headquarters in Germany. So they entered into the study of the language with an enthusiasm and perseverance that insured progress. There was a German nurse for the children, and the whole atmosphere of the household presently became lingually Teutonic. It amused Mark Twain, as everything amused him, but he was a good student; he acquired a working knowledge of the language in an extraordinarily brief time, just as in an earlier day he had picked up piloting. He would never become a German scholar, but his vocabulary and use of picturesque phrases, particularly those that combined English and German words, were often really startling, not only for their humor, but for their expressiveness. *(2)*

Drat this German tongue, I never shall be able to learn it. I think I could learn a little conversational stuff, maybe, if I could attend to it, but I found I couldn't spare the time. I took lessons two weeks & got so I could understand the talk going on around me, & even answer back, after a fashion. But I neither talk nor listen, now, so I can't even understand the language any more. Mrs. Clemens is getting along fast, & Miss Spaulding & our little Susie talk the devilish tongue without difficulty. *(7)*

German language is a dozen fragments of words flung into an octagonal cylinder – take a good look at them before you begin to turn the machine, for you will never see them in their simplicity again – never never any more. TURN! – <up flashes> up spring your fragmental elements with Ver's & Be's & Ge's & Er's & lein's & schen's & gung's & heits & keits & zu's & a thousand other flashing & blazing prefixes, affixes & interjections broidered <in> on them or hung to them. – Turn & turn! the combinations will be infinite, & bewilwilderingly enchanting & magnificent – but *these,* also, like the original fragments you shall see but once, then lose them forever. The patterns in this linguistic kaleidoscope are never repeated. *(1)*

Dreamed all bad foreigners went to German heaven, couldn't speak the language, and wished they'd gone to the other place. *(13)*

In early times some sufferer had to sit up with a toothache, and he put in the time inventing the German language.

To make a German sentence complete and beautiful you have only to add: "Wollen haben sollen werden," after you have got through with what you wanted to say. *(1)*

Told 2 German gentlemen the way to the Wolfsbrunnen, in elaborate German – 1 put up his hands & solemnly said, "Gott im Himmel!" *(1)*

However, it is not well to dwell too much on the separable verbs. One is sure to lose his temper early and if he sticks to the subject and will not be warned, it will at last either soften his brain or petrify it. Personal pronouns and adjectives are a fruitful nuisance in this language and should have been left out. For instance, the same sound, *sie*, means *you* and it means *she* and it means *her* and it means *it* and it means *they* and it means *them.* Think of the ragged poverty of a language which has to make one word do the work of six – and a poor little weak thing of only three letters at that. But mainly think of the exasperation of never knowing which of these meanings the speaker is trying to convey. This explains why, whenever a person says *sie* to me, I generally try to kill him, if a stranger.

Now observe the Adjective. Here was a case where simplicity would have been an advantage. Therefore, for no other reason, the inventor of this language complicated it all he could. When we wish to speak of our "good friend or friends" in our enlightened tongue we stick to the one form and have no trouble or hard feeling about it but with the German tongue it is different. When a German gets his hands on an adjective he declines it and keeps on declining it until the common sense is all declined out of it. It is as bad as Latin. He says, for instance:

SINGULAR

Nominative – Mein gut*er* Freund, my good friend.
Genitive – Mein*es* gut*en* Freund*es*, of my good friend.
Dative – Mein*em* gut*en* Freund, to my good friend.
Accusative – Mein*en* gut*en* Freund, my good friend.

PLURAL

N. – Mein*e* gut*en* Freunde, my good friends.
G. – Mein*er* gut*en* Freunde, of my good friends.
D. – Mein*en* gut*en* Freund*en*, to my good friends.
A. – Mein*e* gut*en* Freund*e*, my good friends.

Now let the candidate for the asylum try to memorize those variations and see how soon he will be elected. One might better go without friends in Germany than thake all this trouble about them. I have shown what a bother it is to decline a good (male) friend. Well, this is only a third of the work, for there is a variety of new distortions of the adjective to be learned when the object is feminine, and still another when the object is neuter. Now there are more adjectives in this language than there are black cats in Switzerland and they must all

Aug 8 Very sweet girl in train – Joe told me so in German, to keep her from understanding. This is very neat. Most G's *do* understand English, but very few of them can understand our German. *(1)*

With prayer & a dictionary one may wade through most any sentence *(1)*

He said that when it came to declining a German ----- / verb? he could as easily (or would as soon) decline a drink. – Or, he would rather decline 2 drinks than one German verb. *(1)*

Now there is that <confounded> blistered word Vermählt. I never know whether it means despised, <married,> painted, or suspected. – (Yes, it is married.) *(1)*

German good-society conversation, in which both sexes say Lord God, how good it is! Jesus C! By God! Est ist verdammt gut! (the soup) D–d good. – Said by a lady. *(1)*

Never knew before what Eternity was made for. It is to give some of us a chance to learn German. *(1)*

John Hay, attempting German with a stranger all day, on a diligence – finally stranger, after trying for 20 minutes to form a sentence, said, "Oh, God damn the language!" Hay – embracing him, "Bless my soul you speak English!" *(2)*

John says let a man post himself thoroughly in Zug & Schlag, & then throw in aufheben for style & ornament & you are qualified to carry on a German conversation on any sub- without fear. Yes, sir, then you've got a command of language which places you forever out of trouble. *(1)*

Barring spelling & pronouncing, one ought to learn English in 30 hours – French in 30 days, G in 30 yrs. *(1)*

A dog is "der Hund"; a woman is "die Frau"; a horse is "das Pferd"; now you put that dog in the genitive case, and is he the same dog he was before? No, sir; he is "des Hundes"; put him in the dative case and what is he? Why, he is "dem Hund." Now you snatch him into the accusative case and how is it with him? Why, he is "den Hunden." But suppose he happened to be twins and you have to pluralize him – what then? Why, they'll swat that twin dog around through the 4 cases until he'll think he's an entire inter-national dog-show all in his own person. I don't like dogs, but I wouldn't treat a dog like that – I wouldn't even treat a borrowed dog that way. Well, it's just the same with a cat. They start her in at the nominative singular in good health and fair to look upon, and they sweat her through all the 4 cases and the 16 the's and when she limps out through the accusative plural you wouldn't recognize her for the same being. Yes, sir, once the German language gets hold of a cat it's good-bye cat. That's about the amount of it. *(13)*

be as elaborately declined as the examples above suggested. Difficult? – troublesome? – these words cannot describe it. I heard a Californian student in Heidelberg say in one of his calmest moods that he would rather decline two drinks than one German adjective.

The inventor of the language seems to have taken pleasure in complicating it in every way he could think of. For instance, if one is casually referring to a house, *Haus,* or a horse, *Pferd,* or a dog, *Hund,* he spells these words as I have indicated but if he is referring to them in the Dative case he sticks on a foolish and unneccessary *e* and spells them *Hause, Pferde, Hunde.* So, as an added *e* often signifies the plural, as the *s* does with us, the new student is likely to go on for a month making twins out of a Dative dog before he discovers his mistake. And on the other hand, many a new student who could ill afford loss has bought and paid for two dogs and only got one of them, because he ignorantly bought that dog in the Dative singular when he really supposed he was talking plural – which left the law on the seller's side, of course, by the strict rules of grammar, and therefore a suit for recovery could not lie.

In German all the Nouns begin with a capital letter. Now that is a good idea, and a good idea in this language is necessarily conspicuous from its lonesomeness. I consider this capitalizing of nouns a good idea because by reason of it you are almost always able to tell a noun the minute you see it. You fall into error occasionally because you mistake the name of a person for the name of a thing and waste a good deal of time trying to dig a meaning out of it. German names almost always do mean something and this helps to deceive the student. I translated a passage one day, which said that "the infuriated tigress broke loose and utterly ate up the unfortunate fir forest" *(Tannenwald).* When I was girding up my loins to doubt this, I found out that Tannenwald in this instance was a man's name.

Every noun has a gender and there is no sense or system in the distribution, so the gender of each must be learned separately and by heart. There is no other way. To do this one has to have a memory like a memorandum-book. In German a young lady has no sex, while a turnip has. Think what overwrought reverence that shows for the turnip and what callous disrespect for the girl. See how it looks in print – I translate this from a conversation in one of the best of the German Sunday-school books:

"*Gretchen.* – Wilhelm, where is the turnip?

"*Wilhelm.* – She has gone to the kitchen.

"*Gretchen.* – Where is the accomplished and beautiful English maiden?

"*Wilhelm* – It has gone to the opera."

[Written in 1898. Vienna]

BEAUTIES OF THE GERMAN LANGUAGE. *February 3.* – Lectured for the benefit of a charity last night, in the Börsendorfersaal. Just as I was going on the platform a messenger delivered to me an envelope with my name on it, and this written under it: "Please read one of these to-night." Inclosed were a couple of newspaper clippings – two versions of an anecdote, one German, the other English. I was minded to try the German one on those people, just to see what would happen, but my courage weakened when I noticed the formidable look of the closing word, and I gave it up. A pity, too, for it ought to read well on the platform and get an encore. That or a brickbat. There is never any telling what a new audience will do; their tastes are capricious. The point of this anecdote is a justifiable gibe at the German long word, and is not as much of an exaggeration as one might think. The German long word is not a legitimate construction, but an ignoble artificiality, a sham. It has no recognition by the dictionary and is not found there. It is made by jumbling a lot of words into one, in a quite unnecessary way; it is a lazy device of the vulgar and a crime against the language. Nothing can be gained, no valuable amount of space saved, by jumbling the following words together on a visting card: "Mrs. Smith, widow of the late Commander-in-chief of the Police Department," yet a German widow can persuade herself to do it, without much trouble: "Mrs.-late-commander-in-chief-of-the-police-department's-widow-Smith." This is the English version of the anecdote:

A Dresden paper, the *Weidmann*, which thinks that there are kangaroos (Beutelratte) in South Africa, says the Hottentots (Hottentoten) put them in cages (kotter) provided with covers (lattengitter) to protect them from the rain. The cages are therefore called lattengitterwetterkotter, and the imprisoned kangaroo lattengitterwetterkotterbeutelratte. One day an assassin (attentäter) was arrested who had killed a Hottentot woman (Hottentotenmutter), the mother of two stupid and stuttering children in Strottertrotel. This woman, in the German language is entitled Hottentotenstrottertrottelmutter, and her assassin takes the name Hottentotenstrottermutterattentäter. The murderer was confined in a kangaroo's cage – Beutelrattenlattengitterwetterkotter – whence a few days later he escaped, but fortunately he was recaptured by a Hottentot, who presented himself at the mayor's office with beaming face. "I have captured the Beutelratte," said he. "Which one?" said the mayor; "we have several." "The Attentäterlattengitterwetterkotterbeutelratte." "Which attentäter are you talking about?" "About the Hottentotenstrottertrottelmutterattentäter." "Then why don't you say at once the Hottentotenstrottelmutterattentäterlattengitterwetterkotterbeutelratte?" *(8)*

I am going *in der* Sweitz.
No, in die Sweitz (movement
It is very pretty in die Sweitz
No, *in der* Sweitz. (quiet) *(1)*

Said he – "Mein Fämilienigenthümlichkeiten –"
Said I – "Life is short. I'll have to get you to abbreviate some of your words." *(1)*

To continue with the German genders: a tree is male, its buds are female, its leaves are neuter. Horses are sexless, dogs are male, cats are female – tomcats included, of course. A person's mouth, neck, bosom, elbows, finger, nails, feet and body are of the male sex, and his head is male or neuter according to the word selected to signify it and *not* according to the sex of the individual who wears it – for in Germany all the women wear either male heads or sexless ones. A person's nose, lips, shoulders, breast, hands and toes are of the female sex and his hair, ears, eyes, chin, legs, knees, heart and conscience haven't any sex at all. The inventor of the language probably got what he knew about a conscience from hearsay.

Now, by the above dissection the reader will see that in Germany a man may *think* he is a man but when he comes to look into the matter closely he is bound to have his doubts. He finds that in sober truth he is a most ridiculous mixture. And if he ends by trying to comfort himself with the thought that he can at least depend on a third of this mess as being manly and masculine the humiliating second thought will quickly remind him that in this respect he is no better off than any woman or cow in the land.

In the German it is true that by some oversight of the inventor of the language a Woman is a female but a Wife *(Weib)* is not – which is unfortunate. A Wife here has no sex. She is neuter. So, according to the grammar, a fish is *he*, his scales are *she* but a fishwife is neither. To describe a wife as sexless may be called under-description. That is bad enough, but over-description is surely worse. A German speaks of an Englishman as the *Engländer*. To change the sex he adds *inn*, and that stands for Englishwoman – *Engländerinn*. That seems descriptive enough but still it is not exact enough for a German, so he precedes the word with that article which indicates that the creature to follow is feminine, and writes it down thus: "*die* Engländer*inn*," – which means "the *she*-Englishwoman.*" I consider that that person is over-described.

Well, after the student has learned the sex of a great number of nouns he is still in a difficulty because he finds it impossible to persuade his tongue to refer to things as "*he*" and "*she*" and "*him*" and "*her*," which it has been always accustomed to refer to as "*it*." When he even frames a German sentence in his mind, with the hims and hers in the right places, and then works up his courage to the utterance-point, it is no use – the moment he begins to speak his tongue flies the track and all those labored males and females come out as "*its*." And even when he is reading German to himself he always calls those things "*it*," whereas he ought to read in this way:

Tale of the Fishwife and Its Sad Fate*

It is a bleak Day. Hear the Rain, how he pours, and the Hail, how he rattles, and see the Snow, how he drifts along, and oh the Mud, how deep he is! Ah the poor Fishwife, it is stuck fast in the Mire, it has dropped its Basket of Fishes, and its Hands have been cut by the Scales as it seized some of the falling Creatures, and one Scale has even got into its Eye, and it cannot get her out. It opens its Mouth to cry for Help but if any Sound comes out of him, alas he is drowned by the raging of the Storm. And now a Tomcat has got one of the Fishes and she will surely escape with him. No, she bites off a Fin, she holds her in her Mouth – will she swallow her? No, the Fishwife's brave Mother-dog deserts his Puppies and rescues the Fin – which he eats, himself, as his Reward. O, horror, the Lightning has struck the Fish-basket. He sets him on Fire. See the Flame, how she licks the doomed Utensil with her red and angry Tongue. Now she attacks the helpless Fishwife's Foot – she burns him up, all but the big Toe, and even *she* is partly consumed. And still she spreads, still she waves her fiery Tongues. She attacks the Fishwife's Leg and destroys *it*. She attacks its Hand and destroys *her*. She attacks its poor worn Garment and destroys *her* also. She attacks its Body and consumes *him*. She wreathes herself about its Heart and *it* is consumed. Next about its Breast, and in a Moment *she* is a Cinder. Now she reaches its Neck – *he* goes. Now its Chin – *it* goes. Now its Nose – *she* goes. In another Moment, except Help come, the Fishwife will be no more. Time presses – is there none to succor and save? Yes! Joy, joy, with flying Feet the she-Englishwoman comes! But alas, the generous she-Female is too late: where now is the fated Fishwife! It has ceased from its Sufferings, it has gone to a better Land. All that is left of it for its loved Ones to lament over is this poor smoldering Ash-heap. Ah, woeful, woeful Ash-heap! Let us take him up tenderly, reverently, upon the lowly Shovel and bear him to his long Rest, with the Prayer that when he rises again it will be in a Realm where he will have one good square responsible Sex and have it all to himself instead of having a mangy lot of assorted Sexes scattered all over him in Spots.

There, now, the reader can see for himself that this pronoun business is a very awkward thing for the unaccustomed tongue.

I suppose that in all languages the similarities of look and sound between words which have no similarity in meaning are a fruitful source of perplexity to the foreigner. It is so in our tongue and it is notably the case in the German.

---

* *I capitalize the nouns in the German (and ancient English) fashion.*

Now there is that troublesome word *vermählt:* to me it has so close a resemblance – either real or fancied – to three or four other words that I never know whether it means despised, painted, suspected or married; until I look in the dictionary and then I find it means the latter. There are lots of such words and they are a great torment. To increase the difficulty there are words which *seem* to resemble each other and yet do not but they make just as much trouble as if they did. For instance, there is the word *vermiethen* (to let, to lease, to hire) and the word *verheirathen* (another way of saying to *marry*). I heard of an Englishman who knocked at a man's door in Heidelberg and proposed, in the best German he could command, to *"verheirathen"* that house. Then there are some words which mean one thing when you emphasize the first syllable but mean something very different if you throw the emphasis on the last syllable. For instance, there is a word which means a runaway, or the act of glancing through a book, according to the placing of the emphasis, and another word which signifies to *associate* with a man or to *avoid* him, according to where you put the emphasis – and you can generally depend on putting it in the wrong place and getting into trouble.

There are some exceedingly useful words in this language. *Schlag,* for example, and *Zug.* There are three-quarters of a column of *Schlags* in the dictionary and a column and a half of *Zugs.* The word *Schlag* means Blow, Stroke, Dash, Hit, Shock, Clap, Slap, Time, Bar, Coin, Stamp, Kind, Sort, Manner, Way, Apoplexy, Wood-cutting, Inclosure, Field, Forest-clearing. This is its simple and *exact* meaning – that is to say, its restricted, its fettered meaning. But there are ways by which you can set it free so that it can soar away, as on the wings of the morning, and never be at rest. You can hang any word you please to its tail, and make it mean anything you want to. You can begin with *Schlag-ader,* which means artery, and you can hang on the whole dictionary, word by word, clear through the alphabet to *Schlag-wasser,* which means bilge-water – and including *Schlag-mutter,* which means mother-in-law.

Just the same with *Zug.* Strictly speaking, *Zug* means Pull, Tug, Draught, Procession, March, Progress, Flight, Direction, Expedition, Train, Caravan, Passage, Stroke, Touch, Line, Flourish, Trait of Character, Feature, Lineament, Chess-move, Organ-stop, Team, Whiff, Bias, Drawer, Propensity, Inhalation, Disposition. But that thing which it does *not* mean – when all its legitimate pennants have been hung on – has not been discovered yet.

One cannot overestimate the usefulness of *Schlag* and *Zug.* Armed just with these two and the word *Also,* what cannot the foreigner on German soil accomplish? The German word *Also* is the equivalent of the English phrase "You know" and does not mean anything at all – in *talk,* though it sometimes does in print. Every time a German opens its mouth an *Also* falls out and every time he shuts it he bites one in two that was trying to *get* out.

Now, the foreigner, equipped with these three noble words, is master of the situation. Let him talk right along, fearlessly. Let him pour his indifferent German forth, and when he lacks for a word let him heave a *Schlag* into the vacuum. All the chances are that it fits it like a plug but if it doesn't, let him promptly heave a *Zug* after it. The two together can hardly fail to bung the hole. But if, by a miracle, they *should* fail, let him simply say *Also!* and this will give him a moment's chance to think of the needful word. In Germany, when you load your conversational gun it is always best to throw in a *Schlag* or two and a *Zug* or two, because it doesn't make any difference how much the rest of the charge may scatter, you are bound to bag something with *them.* Then you blandly say *Also* and load up again. Nothing gives such an air of grace and elegance and unconstraint to a German or an English conversation as to scatter it full of "Also's" or "You-knows."

In my note-book I find this entry:

July 1. – In the Hospital yesterday a word of thirteen syllables was successfully removed from a patient – a North-German from near Hamburg. But as most unfortunately the surgeons had opened him in the wrong place, under the impression that he contained a panorama, he died. The sad event has cast a gloom over the whole community.

That paragraph furnishes a text for a few remarks about one of the most curious and notable features of my subject – the length of German words. Some German words are so long that They have a perspective. Observe these examples:

FREUNDSCHAFTSBEZEIGUNGEN.

DILETTANTENAUFDRINGLICHKEITEN.

STADTVERORDNETENVERSAMMLUNGEN.

These things are not words, they are alphabetical processions. And they are not rare. One can open a German newspaper any time and see them marching majestically across the page – and if he has any imagination he can see the banners and hear the music, too. They impart a martial thrill to the meekest subject. I take a great interest in these curiosities. Whenever I come across a good one I stuff it and put it in my museum. In this way I have made quite a valuable collection. When I get duplicates, I exchange with other collectors and thus increase the variety of my stock. Here are some specimens which I lately bought at an auction sale of the effects of a bankrupt bric-à-brac hunter:

GENERALSTAATSVERORDNETENVERSAMMLUNGEN.

ALTERTHUMSWISSENSCHAFTEN.

KINDERBEWAHRUNGSANSTALTEN.

UNABHAENGIGKEITSERKLAERUNGEN.

WIEDERERSTELLUNGSBESTREBUNGEN.

WAFFENSTILLSTANDSUNTERHANDLUNGEN.

Of course when one of these grand mountain ranges goes stretching across the printed page, it adorns and ennobles that literary landscape – but at the same time it is a great distress to the new student, for it blocks up his way. He cannot crawl under it or climb over it or tunnel through it. So he resorts to the dictionary for help, but there is no help there. The dictionary must draw the line somewhere – so it leaves this sort of words out. And it is right, because these long things are hardly legitimate words but are rather combinations of words, and the inventor of them ought to have been killed. They are compound words with the hyphens left out. The various words used in building them are in the dictionary but in a very scattered condition. So you can hunt the materials out one by one and get at the meaning at last but it is a tedious and harrassing business. I have tried this process upon some of the above examples. *Freundschaftsbezeigungen*" seems to be "Friendship demonstrations," which is only a foolish and clumsy way of saying "demonstrations of friendship." "*Unabhaengigkeitserklaerungen*" seems to be "Independencedeclarations," which is no improvement upon "Declarations of Independence," so far as I can see. "*Generalstaatsverordnetenversammlungen*" seems to be "Generalstatesrepresentativesmeetings," as nearly as I can get at it – a mere rhythmical, gushy euphuism for "meetings of the legislature," I judge. We used to have a good deal of this sort of crime in our literature but it has gone out now. We used to speak of a thing as a "never-to-be-forgotten" circumstance, instead of cramping it into the simple and sufficient word "memorable" and then going calmly about our business as if nothing had happened. In those days we were not content to embalm the thing and bury it decently, we wanted to build a monument over it.

But in our newspapers the compounding-disease lingers a little to the present day, but with the hyphens left out, in the German fashion. This is the shape it takes: instead of saying "Mr. Simmons, clerk of the county and district courts, was in town yesterday," the new form puts it thus: "Clerk of the County and Districts Courts Simmons was in town yesterday." This saves neither time nor ink and has an awkward sound besides. One often sees a remark like this in our papers: "*Mrs.* Assistant District Attorney Johnson returned to her city residence yesterday for the season." That is a case of really unjustifiable compounding, because it not only saves no time or trouble but confers a title on Mrs. Johnson which she has no right to. But these little instances are trifles indeed contrasted with the ponderous and dismal German system of piling jumbled compounds together. I wish to submit the following local item from a Mannheim journal by way of illustration:

"In the daybeforeyesterdayshortlyaftereleveno'clock Night, the inthistown-standingtavern called 'The Wagoner' was down-burnt. When the fire to the onthedownburninghousecresting Stork's Nest reached, flew the parent Storks away. But when the bytheraging, firesurrounded Nest *itself* caught Fire, straightway plunged the quickreturning Mother-stork into the Flames and died, her Wings over her young ones outspread."

Even the cumbersome German construction is not able to take the pathos out of that picture – indeed it somehow seems to strengthen it. This item is dated away back yonder months ago. I could have used it sooner but I was waiting to hear from the Father-stork. I am still waiting.

"Also!" If I have not shown that the German is a difficult language, I have at least intented to do it. I have heard of an American student who was asked how he was getting along with his German and who answered promptly: "I am not getting along at all. I have worked at it hard for three level months and all I have got to show for it is one solitary German phrase – *'Zwei glas'*" (two glasses of beer). He paused a moment, reflectively, then added with feeling· "But I've got that *solid!*"

And if I have not also shown that German is a harassing and infuriating study, my execution has been at fault, and not my intent. I heard lately of a worn and sorely tried American student who used to fly to a certain German word for relief when he could bear up under his aggravations no longer – the only word in the whole language whose sound was sweet and precious to his ear and healing to his lacerated spirit. This was the word *Damit*. It was only the *sound* that helped him, not the meaning.* And so, at last, when he learned that the emphasis was not on the first syllable, his only stay and support was gone and he faded away and died.

I think that a description of any loud, stirring, tumultuous episode must be tamer in German than in English. Our descriptive words of this character have such a deep, strong, resonant sound, while their German equivalents do seem so thin and mild and energyless. Boom, burst, crash, roar, storm, bellow, blow, thunder, explosion; howl, cry, shout, yell, groan; battle, hell. These are magnificent words. They have a force and magnitude of sound befitting the things which they describe. But their German equivalents would be ever so nice to sing the children to sleep with, or else my awe-inspiring ears were made for display and not for superior usefulness in analyzing sounds. Would any man

---

* *It merely means, in its general sense, "herewith."*

want to die in a battle which was called by so tame a term as a *Schlacht*? Or would not a consumptive feel too much bundled up, who was about to go out, in a shirt-collar and a seal-ring, into a storm which the bird-song word *Gewitter* was employed to describe? And observe the strongest of the several German equivalents for explosion – *Ausbruch*. Our word Toothbrush is more powerful than that. It seems to me that the Germans could do worse than import it into their language to describe particularly tremendous explosions with. The German word for hell – Hölle – sounds more like *helly* than anything else. Therefore, how necessarily chipper, frivolous and unimpressive it is. If a man were told in German to go there, could he really rise to the dignity of feeling insulted?

Having pointed out in detail the several vices of this language, I now come to the brief and pleasant task of pointing out its virtues. The capitalizing of the nouns I have already mentioned. But far before this virtue stands another – that of spelling a word according to the sound of it. After one short lesson in the alphabet the student can tell how any German word is pronounced without having to ask, whereas in our language if a student should inquire of us, "What does B, O, W, spell?" we should be obliged to reply, "Nobody can tell what it spells when you set it off by itself. You can only tell by referring to the context and finding out what it signifies – whether it is a thing to shoot arrows with, or a nod of one's head, or the forward end of a boat."

There are some German words which are singularly and powerfully effective. For instance, those which describe lowly, peaceful and affectionate home life. Those which deal with love in any and all forms, from mere kindly feeling and honest good will toward the passing stranger, clear up to courtship. Those which deal with outdoor Nature in its softest and loveliest aspects – with meadows and forests and birds and flowers, the fragrance and sunshine of summer, and the moonlight of peaceful winter nights. In a word, those which deal with any and all forms of rest, repose and peace. Those also which deal with the creatures and marvels of fairyland. And lastly and chiefly, in those words which express pathos is the language surpassingly rich and effective. There are German songs which can make a stranger to the language cry. That shows that the *sound* of the words is correct – it interprets the meanings with truth and with exactness, and so the ear is informed, and through the ear the heart.

The Germans do not seem to be afraid to repeat a word when it is the right one. They repeat it several times if they choose. That is wise. But in English, when we have used a word a couple of times in a paragraph we imagine we are growing tautological and so we are weak enough to exchange it for some other

In Europe they use safety matches and then entrust candles to drunken men, children, idiots, etc., and yet suffer little from fires, apparently. The idea of an open light in one of our houses makes us shudder.

Heard cuckoo in woods at W. May 2. Heinrich said: "How long shall I live?" The cuckoo went on cuckooing for the next 20 minutes – wherefore H. is a Methuselah, each yell meaning a year. First cuckoo I ever heard outside of a clock. Was surprised how closely it imitated the clock – and yet of course it could never have heard a clock. The hatefulest thing in the world is a cuckoo clock. *(13)*

Unberufen! & knock *under* the table or other wood 3 times – the superstition being that the evil spirits hear you say "What fine weather it is!" They will immediately change it unless you ward it off the invocation "Unberufen!" *(1)*

Some of the German words are so long that they have a perspective. When one casts his glance along down one of these it gradually tapers to a point, like the receding lines of a railway track. *(1)*

delighted – "I pricked up my ears & glowed with delight – I doubted my ears – no, it was perfectly true, I was understanding every word he said ------ he was talking English!

(Used to hearing nothing but German, naturally thought they were talking German.) *(1)*

I wish I could hear myself talk German. *(1)*

The chief German characteristic seems to be kindness, good will to men.

(Sweet petting-sounding talk of birds & flowers & leaves & trees & fields – & it is not mere *talk* from a poet's attic, they *do* live in the open air.)

Germans comb their hair in public and have some other little peculiarities, but there is one thing which you can charge the entire nation with: ask any German a question and you will get a civil answer.

Would like to have 2 monopolies [–] umbrellas in England & specs here. I would rather be a spectacle-maker in Germany than anything else. – These people might possibly get along without clothes, or Bibles, or even beer, but they've got to have spectacles.

When 12 or 13 Germans are gathered together, if there be one without glasses, suspect him for a foreigner.

I think that only God can read a German newspaper.

Dreamed all bad foreigners went to German Heaven – couldn't talk & wished they had gone to the other place.

After this German chapter I will now put the remnants of my mind on other things. *(1)*

word which only approximates exactness, to escape what we wrongly fancy is a greater blemish. Repetition may be bad but surely inexactness is worse.

There are people in the world who will take a great deal of trouble to point out the faults in a religion or a language and then go blandly about their business without suggesting any remedy. I am not that kind of a person. I have shown that the German language needs reforming. Very well, I am ready to reform it. At least I am ready to make the proper suggestions. Such a course as this might be immodest in another. But I have devoted upward of nine full weeks, first and last, to a careful and critical study of this tongue and thus have acquired a confidence in my ability to reform it which no mere superficial culture could have conferred upon me.

In the first place I would leave out the Dative case. It confuses the plurals. And, besides, nobody ever knows when he is in the Dative case except he discover it by accident – and then he does not know when or where it was that he got into it or how long he has been in it or how he is ever going to get out of it again. The Dative case is but an ornamental folly – it is better to discard it.

In the next place I would move the Verb further up to the front. You may load up with ever so good a Verb but I notice that you never really bring down a subject with it at the present German range – you only cripple it. So I insist that this important part of speech should be brought forward to a position where it may be easily seen with the naked eye.

Thirdly, I would import some strong words from the English tongue – to swear with and also to use in describing all sorts of vigorous things in a vigorous way.*

Fourthly, I would reorganize the sexes and distribute them according to the will of the Creator. This as a tribute of respect, if nothing else.

Fifthly, I would do away with those great long compounded words or require the speaker to deliver them in sections, with intermissions for refreshments. To wholly do away with them would be best, for ideas are more easily received and digested when they come one at a time than when they come in bulk. Intellectual food is like any other. It is pleasanter and more beneficial to take it with a spoon than with a shovel.

---

* "Verdammt" and its variations and enlargements are words which have plenty of meaning, but the sounds are so mild and ineffectual that German ladies can use them without sin. German ladies who could not be induced to commit a sin by any persuasion or compulsion promptly rip out one of these harmless little words when they tear their dresses or don't like the soup. It sounds about as wicked as our "My gracious." German ladies are constantly saying, "Ach! Gott!" "Mein Gott!" "Gott in Himmel!" "Herr Gott!" "Der Herr Jesus!" etc. They think our ladies have the same custom, perhaps, for I once heard a gentle and lovely old German lady say to a sweet young American girl: "The two languages are so alike – how pleasant that is. We say 'Ach Gott!' you say 'Goddam.'"

Sixthly, I would require a speaker to stop when he is done and not hang a string of those useless *"haben sind gewesen gehabt haben geworden seins"* to the end of his oration. This sort of gewgaws undignify a speech instead of adding a grace. They are therefore an offense and should be discarded.

Seventhly, I would discard the Parenthesis. Also the reparenthesis, the re-reparenthesis and the re-re-re-re-re-reparenthesis, and likewise the final wide-reaching all-inclosing king-parenthesis. I would require every individual, be he high or low, to unfold a plain straightforward tale or else coil it and sit on it and hold his peace. Infractions of this law should be punishable with death.

And eightly, and last, I would retain *Zug* and *Schlag* with their pendants and discard the rest of the vocabulary. This would simplify the language.

My philological studies have satisfied me that a gifted person ought to learn English (barring spelling and pronouncing) in thirty hours, French in thirty days and German in thirty years. It seems manifest, then, that the latter tongue ought to be trimmed down and repaired. If it is to remain as it is it ought to be gently and reverently set aside among the dead languages, for only the dead have time to learn it.

APPENDICE

GIs Drink Deep at a Fount of Beer—and Learning

Maybe in Heidelberg They Spell Kultur With a 'C'

By Howard Byrne

Stars and Stripes Staff Writer

HEIDELBERG, Germany, Apr. 2— An American tank crew sitting on the tank in front of the University of Heidelberg seemed rather unimpressed with its dimensions.

"I heard a lot about that place," said S/Sgt. Charles Phillips, of Meriden, Miss. "It ain't much to look at, is it?"

It wasn't. Almost any college at home could put the University of Heidelberg in its back pocket. Yet these small austere buildings had been the alma mater for the bulk of the German General Staff officers, and many Nazi party leaders.

The doughboys of the 63rd Division, which took the town after crossing the Neckar River while the 10th Armored Division pushed around it, seemed better acquainted with Heidelberg as the home of good beer than as a seat of learning. They weren't getting any of it, though. The shipping platform of one brewery was stacked with barrels, but a sign said "Off Limits."

All Taverns Shut Down

Taverns in the town were all closed and were also verboten. The doughboys hoped someone would work out a deal so they could taste the famous brew just so they could boast about it later. (Picture, right, indicates some of them succeeded.)

They didn't expect to be hanging around long. They hadn't been stopping much lately. Heidelberg, with its lush shop windows jammed with fine merchandise, drew their caustic comment. Even during the war, Heidelberg must have been a snug, secure retreat for those who had money.

"These Germans really had it made," said Jack Hoverton, of Louisville, Ky.

Immaculate Heidelberg contrasts sharply with nearby Kaiserslautern, Mannheim and Worms, all of which look like garbage dumps. Maj. Lee Plummer, military government officer, explained that Allied airmen rarely made Heidelberg a target and American divisions which took the town were purposly sparing with their artillery. It was like firing at Princeton or Cambridge.

All of Heidelberg's 100,000 wellgroomed men and modish women were standing on corners watching the Americans enter. They did not betray the uneasiness one sees in the villages where the people believe the Americans will kill them.

Heidelberg knows from experience that the Americans are kindly people. They only have to look at their own hospitals and cultural centers. Many of them were endowed by American philanthropists.

MARK TWAIN IN EUROPE 1878/79

The itinerary of the 1878/1879 European trip follows. The excursions which Clemens and Twichell made without the other members of the party have been marked with asterisks.

11 April 1878	*Holsatia* sails from New York
25 - [30] April	Hamburg
[1 - 3] May	To Cassel, via Hanover and Göttingen; excursion to Wilhelmshöhe
4 May	Frankfort on the Main
6 May - 23 July	Heidelberg
24 May	Excursion to Mannheim
30 May	Excursion to Mannheim
10 July	Excursion to Worms
23 July	To Baden-Baden
24 - [27] July	Black Forest
6 August	* Back to Heidelberg, via Oppenau
8 August	* To Heilbronn
9 August	* Neckar boat trip from Heilbronn to Hirschhorn
10 August	* Return to Baden-Baden
Sept., Oct., Nov.	Switzerland, Italy
15 Nov. 1878 - 27 Feb. 1879	Munich
March - July	Paris, France
15 July	Amsterdam
28 - 28 July	London
29 July - 20 August	Oxford, Lake District
21 August	Arrive in Liverpool
23 August	S.S. *Gallia* sails from Liverpool
3 September	Arrival in New York; leave

Mark Twain: "The first thing to remind us we were out of Germany was the sign in depot beyond the Rhine in Switzerland:

'Vor Taschendieben wird gewarnt. Méfiez vous des Voleurs. Beware of Pickpockets.'"

TWAIN ON EUROPE IN GENERAL

For good or for evil we continue to educate Europe. We have held the post of instructor for more than a century and a quarter now. We were not elected to it, we merely took it. We are of the Anglo-Saxon race.

Our public motto is "In God we trust," and when we see those gracious words on the trade-dollar (worth sixty cents) they always seem to tremble and whimper with pious emotion. That is our public motto. It transpires that our private one is, "When the Anglo-Saxon wants a thing *he just takes it.*" Our public morals are touchingly set forth in that stately and yet gentle and kindly motto which indicates that we are a nation of gracious and affectionate multitudinous brothers compacted into one – *"e pluribus unum."* Our private morals find the light in the sacred phrase, "Come, *step* lively!"

We imported our imperialism from monarchical Europe, also our curious notions of patriotism – that is, if we have any principle of patriotism which any person can definitely and intelligibly define. It is but fair then, no doubt, that we should instruct Europe in return for these and the other kinds of instruction which we have received from that source.

Something more than a century ago we gave Europe the first notions of liberty it had ever had and thereby largely and happily helped to bring on the French Revolution and claim a share in its beneficent results. We have taught Europe many lessons since. But for us, Europe might never have known the interviewer; but for us certain of the European states might never have experienced the blessing of extravagant imposts; but for us the European Food Trust might never have acquired the art of poisoning the world for cash; but for us her Insurance Trusts might never have found out the best way to work the widow and orphan for profit; but for uns the long delayed resumption of Yellow Journalism in Europe might have been postponed for generations to come. Steadily, continuously, persistently, we are Americanizing Europe, and all in good time we shall get the job perfected. *(4)*

*

Europe has lived a life of hypocrisy for ages; it is so ingrained in flesh and blood that sincere speech is impossible to these people, when speaking of hereditary power. "God Save the King" is uttered millions of times a day in Europe, and issues nearly always from just the mouth, neither higher nor lower.

The first gospel of all monarchies should be Rebellion; the second should be Rebellion; and the third and all gospels and the only gospel in any monarchy should be Rebellion against Church and State. *(13)*

COMING BACK 1891

They returned to Germany at the end of August, to Nuremberg, which he notes as the "city of exquisite glimpses," and to Heidelberg, where they had their old apartment of thirteen years before, Room 40 at the Schloss Hotel, with its wonderful prospect of wood and hill, and the haze-haunted valley of the Rhine.

"Went up to Königstuhl, and recognized old Gretchen – the two girls seem to recognize me (gave me hopes) but didn't; two red-headed children I attributed to the younger (fat) one. I was a skittish young thing of 42 in those days." *(13)*

MARK TWAIN'S BOOKS IN GERMANY

The great bulk of the German public became acquainted with Mark Twain through the translations.

In analyzing the factors that explain Mark Twain's reception in Germany in these early years one must not forget the importance of his first visit, in 1878. Paine gives an interesting description of his sojourn in Germany and Switzerland. Wherever he went, we are told, Mark Twain was the center of attraction. The warm affection which he displayed towards the Germans was returned by them. But whether this interest in his person led to a corresponding interest in his books cannot be definitely determined; it is plausible to assume that it did in some instances. One fact, however, stands out clearly – the name of Mark Twain became known to an increasingly larger circle.

It is practically impossible to ascertain the exact number of Mark Twain's books which have been published and circulated in Germany. According to information supplied the writer, many of the publishing firms have gone out of business. Others have destroyed their records, while still others refused to release their data. Nevertheless it is possible to hazard a minimum estimate. On the basis of the available figures, German publishers (from 1874-1937) sold at least 425,000 copies fo the *Sketches*, 240,000 of *The Adventures of Tom Sawyer*, 190,000 of *The Adventures of Huckleberry Finn*, 58,000 of *Life on the Missis-*

sippi, 23,000 of *Tom Sawyer Abroad*, 18,000 of *The Man that Corrupted Hadleyburg*, 30,000 of *More Tramps Abroad*, and 34,000 of *A Tramp Abroad*. Adding to these figures at least 8,000 copies more which represent other works – works which appeared in only one edition – it becomes probable that the total number of volumes of Mark Twain's works actually [1940] *sold* in Germany has reached well over a million.

Throughout the centennial appreciations there runs a note of genuine affection, and what one might almost describe as "cordiality under restraint." The German critics, almost without exception, are happy to express their profound gratitude to Mark Twain as one of the few prominent Americans of his time who displayed a real interest in Germany, Austria, and German Switzerland, and a friendship for them. With pardonable pride they recall the unusually considerate attitude of their countries as hosts to this distinguished American on his frequent visits. They are equally proud of the fact that their lands formed a basic source for some of his works. They point to his descriptions in such works as *A Tramp Abroad* as permanent documents of an observing and deeply sympathetic mind. His shrewd understanding of the German national soul, so vividly shown in his praise as well as condemnation of the German character, landscape, and language, contributed considerably, as the critic Thiess expresses it, to setting aside many misconceptions of the world regarding them. In his criticism of the German language, in which he had an inexhaustible interest, he is even credited with having assisted, in his own way, in the evolution of a healthy and sound *Sprachgefühl. (11)*

To this day most of Twain's books are available in German, probably more than in the States.

HEIDELBERG AND THE
UNITED STATES OF AMERICA

Long before the Indians discovered Christopher Columbus on the shores of America, the people of Heidelberg had built the University (in 1386) and the Castle. People had been living here in the times of Christ and probably much earlier, but few of the really old buildings have survived, because a fire and french soldiers tried to destroy the city several times, mainly in the 17th century. Most damage was done in 1693, when only the Hotel Ritter, right next to the market place survived. It looks today as it did in the Middle Ages. Another place that has not changed for a long time is the student pub "Zum Seppl," which serves beer and wine since 1634.

When Columbus met the Indians, Heidelberg was just rebuilding the Castle, the Marstall (next to the river) and the Heilig Geist Kirche were about to be finished building. Twenty years later Martin Luther did visit Heidelberg. 200 years later many citizens of Heidelberg would leave for America, mostly because of religious and financial reasons.

A few years before William Penn founded the city of Philadelphia in 1681 he was preaching near Heidelberg. Around that time, the boom of German emmigrants to the States started. Why did people, even whole families leave their *"Heimat"*? The reasons are still the same today for people from the east or south coming to Germany and to the U.S.A.: political, economical and religious oppressions. The people of Heidelberg had to change their religion up to six times between 1556 and 1685. Everytime the ruler decided to change his church, the people had to follow – from being catholics, to protestants to calvinists and back.

In 1736 40,000 Germans had already landed in Pennsylvania. To this day they are often called "Dutch," even if they were Germans. So big became their number, that Benjamin Franklin wanted them to settle someplace else. Many of them moved to the mid west, but even more kept coming from everywhere, and lots of them from Heidelberg and Palatina. Many of those people could not read and write. Letters to their relatives in Germany had "Pinßel Fania" or "Bünsel Fany" as an address instead of "Pennsylvania."

People were so poor that many didn't survive the trip. Some people from the Odenwald even weren't allowed to leave the ship and were sent right back to Europe (if they survived!) because they had no money and nothing else. The sailing ship trips lasted between 8 and 20 weeks, and the boats carried between 200 and 300 people. Four grown-ups had to share the space of 6 square foot. Most of their possession had to be payed for a "visa." In the city archives of Heidelberg you can still see the original documents from emigrants at that time, for instance how much the Eisenhauers (who became Eisenhowers in Philadelphia) had to pay to get out of this place. The priest Theodor Schneider who used to be head of the University here at that time went to Pennsylvania, as did the mystic Johann Konrad Beissel from Eberbach. He founded a monastery south of Lancaster, which is a museum today. David Ziegler from Heidelberg became the first lord mayor of Cincinnati.

As you can see, many Germans from this area went to the "promised land" – with the exception of catholic women, who were not allowed to enter the

States and got all shipped back. Germans built their own cities, like Allemands near New Orleans and they changed their names: Hershey, Henry, Custer (Küster), Pennybaker, Rice, Rockefeller (Roggenfelder) were originally all German names. Read more about it in the three books by Strassburger and Hinke, "Pennsylvania German Pioneers," which list about 30,000 names only from the time between 1727 and 1775.

Maybe your forefathers (and mothers) were Germans, too?

Today we know of five villages and cities in the U.S.A. called Heidelberg. The biggest one, with a population of more than 70,000 is Heidelberg, Minnesota. Heidelberg, south west of Pittsburgh has a population of 3,500; 5,000 people live in Heidelberg, Mississippi, 870 in Heidelberg, Missouri and only 170 in Heidelberg, Kentucky. There are rumours of several "Heidelbergs" in Canada, but the city archive has no information about them. Until 1941 there was even a Heidelberg near the Black Sea in Russia, but this one has been renamed since.

Nobody knows what made Mark Twain stay in Heidelberg for such a long time. Maybe he was prompted by old dreams from the times he was passing Heidelberg, Mississippi while working on the steamships? Did he plan to stay here or did he and his family just fall in love with this city? Germany at that time was known world-wide as the "hospital of the world," with many American and Russian members of the high society coming here to take a cure at a spa. What we know about Twain's taste in music makes it unlikely that he was attracted by Sigmund Romberg's opera, "The Student Prince," that is still performed in the castle grounds every year. It is performed mostly for Americans, as the opera seems to be better known in the States than in Europe, where it is seen as too much "Kitsch" about the "good old days."

When Twain came to Heidelberg, the city counted some 23,000 souls, less than many Americans living here today! The old "Harbour Square" had just been renamed into Bismarck-Platz, the name that is still used today.

"Mark Twain is probably the only well known American who can be identified with Heidelberg. American residents of Heidelberg planned to erect a monument to Twain here in 1910, but the plan was foiled by World War I. It was made good to some extent after World War II when a US Army residential district here was named Mark Twain Village, and one of its streets, Mark Twain Strasse." *(17)*

The first American to get a honorable citizen award (*"Ehrenbürgerschaft"*) was Jacob Gould Schurman, who helped building the new University building in 1930. More about him elsewhere in this book. Another well-known American who had a special connection with Heidelberg was Major William A.

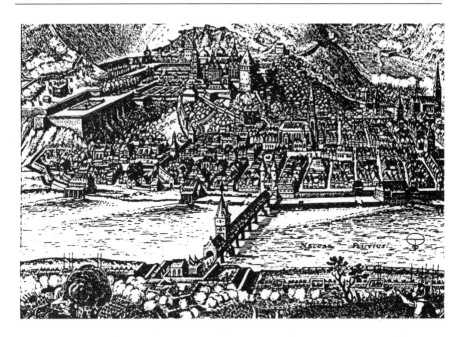

Beiderlinden. In an article in the "Reader's Digest" of 1952 it is claimed that he saved Heidelberg from being bombed in the last days of the 2nd World War. All the cities around Heidelberg (especially Karlsruhe and Mannheim) were completely destroyed, only Heidelberg was saved.

I did some research on that subject for another book ("Heidelberg zur Stunde Null, 1945" – ed. by Werner Pieper, Grubhofer Verlag, Heidelberg, 1985). I found several theories, one as good as the other, but there seems to be no way to tell the definite truth about it. Beiderlinden is today commonly celebrated as the savior of the city – even if there exists no definite proof for that.

Another theory has long been overlooked, but it might as well be the right one. It is definitely my favorite theory: in 1741 some very poor people emigrated from the Odenwald, just 20 miles from Heidelberg, to Philadelphia. Many people emigrated then, but among them was a family that bore a name found only in this area: Eisenhauer (means "iron-miner"). What a coincidence that more than 200 years later the Major General of the Allied Forces in 1945 was General Eisenhower. In the book "President Dwight D. Eisenhowers Ancestors and Relations" (published in 1955) it is proven without doubt that it was really this area that the forefathers of Ike Eisenhower, later President of the United States, came from. No wonder the city was not bombed: he wanted to save his relations.

"He was the youngest son in the family, and as there was no room for him on his father's farm at Eiterbach, where today the column of the well of 1763 has remained, Hans Nicholas left the farm, and most likely earned his living as a weaver or lumberman, or served as a soldier with any of the troop units. About 1712 he got married to a woman whose name we don't know, and with her he had two sons, Johannes and Hans Peter. About 1725 he got married for a second time. His intended wife was Anna Margarethe Strubel, who was born in Lörzenbach in the Odenwald Mountains in 1707. She gave birth to the children Johannes, *24-6-1727, Martin, *1728, and Maria Magdalena, * about 1729/ 30. Together with his wife and his children he emigrated to Pennsylvania in 1741.

"He should not be the only emigrant of his family. His nephew Johann Adam Eisenhauer and his family from Wilhelmsfeld followed him to America in 1751; also Johann Jakob Eisenhauer, entering American soil in 1753, may be counted among this lineage. Eva Eisenhauer, the widow of Johann Leonhard being another nephew of Hans Nicholas, emigrated to Hungaria in 1766. We learn about her nephew Johann Georg Eisenhauer from Altenbach that he furtively ran away in 1772. Among later emigrants of this family there is another Johann Georg Eisenhauer who went to Australia in 1825, whereas Johann Michael Eisenhauer emigrated to USA, his brother Johann Georg, and another Michael Eisenhauer, went to Africa. Thus, members of this family are migrating throughout 5 generations (see the pedigree).

"Consequently Eiterbach in the southern Odenwald is the original home of the President. Up to today you can see the column of the well within the fence of the farm and the descendants still run it.

"Hans Eisenhauer was the emigrant's father, who lived in Heddesbach in 1646, a small village near Heiligkreuzsteinach, and at Eiterbach in 1671. Yet we don't know his ancestors. Adam Eisenhauer, a vine grower, might perhaps be considered as one of his forefathers who lived in Schriesheim at the Bergstraße in 1599, or the miller Hans Eisenhauer, runing the Bergheim mill near Heidelberg in 1568, or most likely that certain Sebaldus Eisenhauer, whose tomb of 1504 we made out in Ober-Mossau, being considered as the oldest Eisenhauer Monument." *(15)*

This theory might be better than others, but nobody knows for sure why the American Army declared Heidelberg as their Headquarters in 1945. I was told that the war diaries of the 7th American Army are lost and can't be found in the Pentagon. Too bad.

In 1945 the army took over several buildings in the city, like the "Landfried Haus," next to the railways station. It used to be a tobacco factory that used local and Turkish tobacco for cigarettes and cigars. Right after the war tobacco was not available for Germans, and for a while American cigarettes became the inofficial currency. Now there was a place in southern Germany where you could get two packages of tobacco – the Landfried Haus in Heidelberg. You had to show papers that proved that you had been a soldier. People came from 200 miles away. They had to walk as there was no public transportation and definitely no cars for Germans at that time. Those guys got their first taste of real Virginia tobacco. Ever since 1945 Germans have smoked American tobacco and not Turkish as they used to. The brand names of cigarettes did not change, only their contents. The local taste in drugs and things that get you hooked also seems to be the result of things brought over by American soldiers: soft and hard drugs in the '60s, Hamburgers, Coke and rock music today.

One of the leading American singer/song-writers, Jackson Browne was born in Heidelberg. The list of his fellow countrymen who came to perform here is too long to be included here. Let's just mention Frank Zappa, Erica Jong, Robert McNamara, Tom Ruddock, Alan Ginsberg, Rudy Rucker, Becky McGhee, Robert Anton Wilson, Timothy Leary…

When the production of the fashion line "Betty Barclay" was stopped in the States, "Betty" came to Heidelberg, where she is still doing OK, giving jobs to more than 2,000 people. The German "Betty Barclay" was founded by Max Berk, who is over 80 years old today. As a hobby he collects textiles from all over the world. Today they are on display in the "Museum of Textile Goods" in Ziegelhausen, just up the river.

The most prominent American feature in Heidelberg is the presence of the American Army.

HISTORY OF THE U.S. MILITARY IN HEIDELBERG

The Heidelberg Military Community encompasses 19 separate installations or "kasernes" in and around Heidelberg – a city largely spared from allied bombing during World War II. Most of the Kasernes were originally built between 1890 and 1939. Building of red sandstone and steeply-pitched gray tile roofs were positioned on a formal grid of streets surrounding a large central parade field. Now, the Heidelberg area serves as Headquarters: U.S. Army, Europe and Seventh Army (HQ USAREUR/7A); the Central Army Group (CENTAG); Fourth Allied Tactical Air Force (4ATAF); and various support groups.

Campbell Barracks. This installation was built in 1937 on what was then farm-land on the southern outskirts of the city, near the village of Rohrbach. The facility was constructed to accomodate the expansion of German armed forces, and was designated as the Grossdeutschland (Greater Germany) Kaserne in March 1938, when Austria was absorbed into the German Empire.

Since Heidelberg survived the war undamaged by allied bombs, Campbell Barracks and other local Kasernes retain a number of relics. The two eagle statues that stand at the gate of Campbell and the four figures that dominate the entrance above the main entry portal on Roemerstrasse, are symbolic for key periods in German history. The far right figure is of a Wuerttemberg Jaeger (infantryman) of 1850; left of him a Hessian of 1806; the next figure represents the late 19th century and German unification, while the figure on the far left represents the 20th century, World War I and Third Reich. Many other bas-relief figures in sandstone showing German soldiers from different periods adorn the entrances of other buildings throughout Campbell.

Mark Twain Village (MTV). Just north of Campbell Barracks is the family housing area of Mark Twain Village, an urban village in the City of Heidelberg. It was named after the 19th Century American writer and satirist in 1958.

Mark Twain travelled widely in Germany and took Heidelberg especially to heart, visiting here nine different times from 1880 to 1907. In "A Tramp Abroad," Twain wrote of his impressions and experiences of German language and customs in the Neckar Valley. Through this book, he introduced thousands of U.S. readers to Heidelberg, and the name "Mark Twain" is nearly as familiar to Germans as to Americans.

130th Station Hospital. One kilometer south of Campbell Barracks is the 130th Station Hospital, which serves American Troops and their family members in the Heidelberg, Mannheim, and Karlsruhe areas. The installation, Nachrichten Kaserne also includes the administrative offices of the Seventh Medical Command.

When American occupation began at the end of World War II, a hospital was organized at this location. Just a few months later, it treated its most famous patient, General George S. Patton. Patton was paralyzed by an automobile accident that occurred near Mannheim in December 1945 and died in the hospital after a two-week struggle. The hospital serves military personal only, there are no facilities for american civilians and/or tourists. There will be help in cases of emergency though.

AMERICA AT THE
TIME OF MARK TWAIN'S VISIT
IN HEIDELBERG

T o broaden the historical perspective, here are some facts about the 1870's: Ulysses S. Grant was President from 1869 to 1877. Read about him and Twain in the beginning of this book in the chapter about the Schloss-Hotel. He was followed as President of the United States by Rutherford B. Hayes, who held office until 1881.

In 1870 the United States had a population of 39,818,499, including almost 5 million freed slaves. The last of the Confederate states were readmitted to the Union, and the 15th amendment, guaranteeing voting rights for all men (but not women!) regardless of "race, color or previous conditions of servitude" was ratified. In 1871 battles between Native Indians and white invaders increased. In 1876 General Custer was defeated and killed in the legendary battle at Little Big Horn in what is now Montana. In the same year Colorado became the 38th state. Also in 1876 the National League of Professional Baseball Clubs was founded. Alexander Graham Bell invented the telephone and one year later Thomas Alva Edison recited "Mary had a little lamb" into his talking machine which became the record player.

MARK TWAIN: MORE NOTES ON GERMANY
(mostly taken out of his Note Books & Journals, Vol II, 1877–1883)

Everywhere the evidences of great freedom & superb government.

From a German paper: "What constitutes official disgrace in America?" *Ans* – God knows.

To have a great crow heave up his shoulders & drop his head between them to look down & scold at me in the solemn mystery of the pines on the Odenwald & say to another crow, O here, this fellow what can he be up to" – it was embarrassing & forced me to move on.

Feeling religious, this morning, I sent a scout to church. He saw the Empress & heard a poor sermon.

Church bells are usually hateful things – these of Heidelberg are also, no doubt, but are softened by distance.

German laundry could not have acquired this perfect ignorance of how to do up a shirt without able instruction – one easily sees England in it. Your collar is like a horse-collar; your shirt can stand alone and when you get into it you feel ready for crime. It is a wonder they do not have more crime here, but it is increasing as adoption of clean shirts spreads among the social democrats.

German cleanliness reaches an altitude to which we may not aspire. These peasants are as cleanly in their houses as the Yankee of romance, and more cleanly than the reality.
 Even in the narrow crooked lanes of the old parts of the cities where the poor dwell, the children are neat and clean – much white stockings on the little girls.

Mr Pfaff – the Americans make things first good, & *then* cheap – but the Germans reverse this.

Street-car conductor wears bright new uniform, & is as polite as – as – but there is nobody at home to compare this politeness with.
 – & politeness costs so little. Our national impoliteness is not natural, but acquired. It would be a curious study, *how* & from whom & why we acquired it.

German hotels and houses are as brilliantly lighted as English ones are dark.

Antique oak chair and table, bought very cheap in Heidelberg. Made last year of pine and stained this year in water-color black which rubs off. Rubbed off all the antiquity in 6 weeks.

ALTERNATIVE
TOURIST & SHOPPING GUIDE

A fter you have dutifully visited the Castle and "done" all the things the official tourist office has told you to do, you may feel like doing something different. If you are into this, read on.

The city's biggest shopping mall is indeed *"Hauptstraße"* where you can buy anything you can buy anywhere else in the world. I suggest you take a different route this time, which might get you closer to the spirit of Mark Twain anyway.

Let's start at the *Holiday Inn,* the former *Hotel Schrieder,* where Twain and his family spent their first night in town. Across the street you'll find the *DAI – Deutsch-Amerikanisches Institut* (Sophienstraße 12, next to the Main Post Office, Tel. 24771). This institute used to be part of the post war re-education program aimed at teaching the Germans democracy. Until a few years ago the institute was still partly financed by the government of the United States; today it is financed by the Germans. They display the latest editions of newspapers and magazines flown in from the states. It houses a big library of books, videos and audio cassettes, shows movies and stages theatre plays, lectures, readings, and expositions. Most of it is free and all of it is in English. The *DAI* carries many of Mark Twain books. It should become one of your favorite spots in town, if you stay more than one week.

Just around the corner in St. Annagasse you will find a beautiful gallery called *"Calumet,"* exhibiting a great collection of modern Indian art, mainly by Hopi and Navajo artists. Tel. 161670. It always reminds me of the visitors from the American Indian Movement in 1973 who supported their struggle in Wounded Knee. Seeing so many GIs in town the Indians said: "It looks just like home." When we told them that we would be happy to see those guys go home the Indians didn't understand: "What do you mean, let them go home? They are back home in Europe where they originally came from. We don't want them back on Turtle-Island!"

OK. Now you find yourself at *"Plöck,"* the parallel street south of the Hauptstraße. It's not so crowded and there a a few specialist shops you might like. Street number 79 is the home of *"Wetzlar,"* a book shop specializing in foreign language books, including a lot of English and American pocket books. It is the place to get some more boks if you like reading while you are traveling. Tel. 24165. Just across the road, *"Lichtblick,"* a new age shop, offers more books, funny postcards, audio cassettes and all the new age paraphernalia which make nice presents. Located at Plöck 46, their telephone is 25963.

If you follow the *Plöck,* you will pass some interesting wine and antique shops. At street number 52, you'll find the most fantastic place to shop, if you got the time. Jürgen's Heidelberger Zuckerladen, an old fashioned shop, with no self service, looks and feels like out of an old time movie. Located between several schools and the University you have to wait up to 30 minutes to get served – but it is well worth it. Jürgen's personal service is the best you can get this side of the Rocky Mountains and his sweets are really sweet. No fotographs please, and take your time.

A side street on the left (*Theaterstraße*) houses the *Deutsch-Amerikanischer Frauenverein,* a second-hand charity shop where you can buy all kinds of cheap priced clothing, books, household goods etc. They even offer second-hand furniture which comes in handy if you stay here for a few months as Mark Twain did.

At the east end of the Plöck is the *Old University Library Building.* A microcosm of time are the medieval handwritings displayed at Heidelberg's university library. The "Manesse Codex" contains the largest known collection of Middle High German lyrical poetry: 426 parchment pages with 6,000 stanzas by 140 poets. The exhibition also includes other famous illustrated handwritings of the "Bibliotheca Palatina", originally in the possesion of the City of Heidelberg, confiscated by Pope Gregory XV in 1623. In 1816, Pope Pius VII returned many of the precious German handwritings to Heidelberg. The exhibition is open Monday through Saturday from 10 a.m. to 5 p.m., from Easter to November 1st, also on Sundays and holidays from 11 a.m. to 4 p.m. (for guided tours call 542539)."

Another good book shop with lots of american books is *Ziehank,* at the Universitätsplatz 12, next to the Library. Just around the corner in the Hauptstraße you will find a *"Bier-Museum"* where you can taste (and get drunk on) more than 100 different beers.

Now you are in the centre of the *Altstadt,* the real Heidelberg, where not much has changed since the times of Mark Twain. There are still countless antique shops, galleries, restaurants, wine bars and shops, and rare book dealers. But not all of it is that old fashioned. For instance there is a wonderful shop for juggling devices, frisbees and other useful things for the traveling person. (*Keule & Co.,* Dreikönigstraße 25, Tel. 12199).

Around that area you will find a few very good take-away restaurants: Chinese, Japanese, and, at *Kornmarkt,* a fantastic vegetarian snack bar, *"Higher*

Taste". The Castle, the Old Bridge and Hotel Ritter are the most famous places
in town, but there are a lot of other walks and buildings which are just as beautiful. Right in the middle of the Altstadt stands the *Heilig Geist Kirche*, the
church Twain wrote about which had a wall in the middle to separate the protestants and catholics. That wall is gone today, but you can still climb up the
church tower. Even if it is not as high as the castle, you have a breathtaking view
over the roofs of the old houses of Heidelberg, the castle, the river...

The Castle is mostly pretty crowded. If you want to take a more quiet walk,
go down to the river near the Congress centre. A small ferry boat will take you
across the Neckar. From the ferry you have a beautiful view up to the Castle,
down the river and to the city itself. If you reach the other side, enjoy the nice
Boat Restaurant on the left or the walk to the right on the *Neckarwiesen*, one
of the best places to be in Heidelberg. You can walk back to the Altstadt,
passing the *Old Bridge*. Goethe said, crossing the river over the Old Bridge,
that is the most beautiful view he had ever encountered. Why not give it a try?
If you feel like taking a longer walk, stay on the other side of the river walk a
few hundred meters up the river to *Hirschgasse*, pass the Hotel where Twain
witnessed the students' duel, walk up the Hirschgasse to the *Hölderlin Memo-
rial*. To the right you can walk for hours in the woods, to the left you will
find yourself on the *Philosophenweg*, the philosopher's walk, with the most
famous view of old Heidelberg. Alan Ginsberg, the American writer and poet,
was so inspired here, that he wrote a poem about it. It was not only the scenic
view which caught his attention, but the industrial landscape and nuclear reac-
tors you can see in the Rhine valley as well:

"HIGHDELBERGH below
orange roofed, misty under grey cloud flowing over oak ridge
across the red stone bridge, over brown Neckar waters
flowing west to the Rhine plains; supporting BASF.
Puffs clouds into blue dusk.
Toilet paper cleenex ninety % of waste
from Mannheim's sixhundredthousand nearby regions.
Laid waste by buildings, but BASF in ninety percent
of the waste reprocess to water-cleaning bacteria plant in the valley.
Illusion of sound of autos in flat space
I scribe above the castle.
Swans on the river by the bridge near the stone wharft
little square holes quayside, empty rainwater
Passers with umbrellas.

Some american drug offenders in the red bricked jail
between the two churches spiring above the roof ridges."

The Philosophenweg runs parallel to the river on the south side of the *Heiligenberg*, the mountain of the holy. It is a steep but rewarding walk. On top of the mountain the Nazis built a huge amphitheatre, holding several thousand people. Once in a while it is still used for classical concerts. As there is not enough parking space it is always problematic to stage big events up there. So the city said "no!" when the Grateful Dead wanted to give a free concert up there in 1972. Behind the amphitheatre are the ruins of the old *Michaelis Basilika,* an old cathedral. If you walk further you have hours and hours of unspoiled woods ahead of you. If you turn around you have a fantastic view down on the Rhine valley, with Mannheim and the mountains on the other side of the valley clearly visible on bright days.

I could go on giving you all kinds of hints, but the best way to get to know a place like Heidelberg is to explore it yourself.

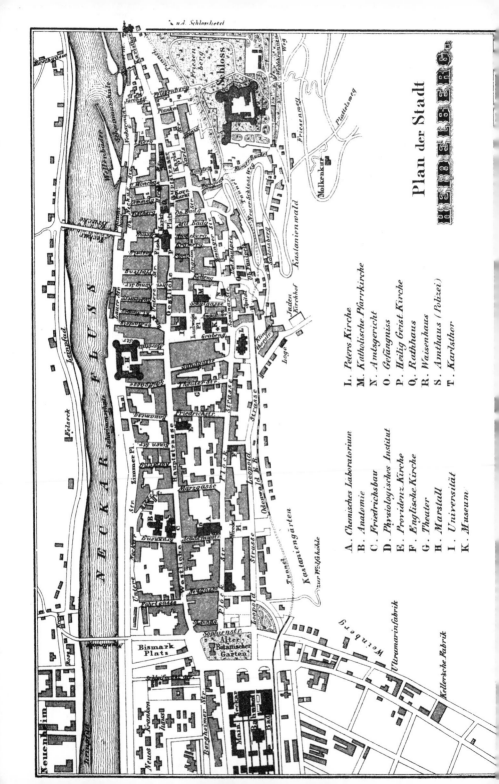

Plan der Stadt
HEIDELBERG

A. Chemisches Laboratorium
B. Anatomie
C. Friedrichsbau
D. Physiologisches Institut
E. Providenz Kirche
F. Englische Kirche
G. Theater
H. Marstall
I. Universität
K. Museum

L. Peters Kirche
M. Katholische Pfarrkirche
N. Amtsgericht
O. Gefängniss
P. Heilig Geist Kirche
Q. Rathhaus
R. Waisenhaus
S. Amthaus (Polizei)
T. Karlsthor

MARK TWAIN'S GUIDE TO HEIDELBERG